Adoptees Come of Age

Counseling and Pastoral Theology

Andrew D. Lester, Series Editor

Adoptees Come
of Age

Living within Two Families

Ronald J. Nydam

Westminster John Knox Press
Louisville, Kentucky

Grateful acknowledgment is made to the following for permission to reprint
previously copyrighted material: University of Notre Dame Press, *Images of Hope:
Imagination as Healer of the Helpless* by William F. Lynch. © 1965 by William F.
Lynch. Used by permission of the publisher.

Book design by Jennifer K. Cox
Cover design by Kevin Derst

First edition
Published by Westminster John Knox Press
Louisville, Kentucky

This book is printed on acid-free paper that meets the
American National Standards Institute Z39.48 standard. ∞

PRINTED IN THE UNITED STATES OF AMERICA
99 00 01 02 03 04 05 06 07 08— 10 9 8 7 6 5 4 3 2 1

Library of Congress Cataloging-in-Publication Data

Nydam, Ronald J.
 Adoptees come of age : living within two families / Ronald J.
Nydam.
  p.   cm. — (Counseling and pastoral theology)
 Includes bibliographical references and index.
 ISBN 0-664-25671-6 (alk. paper)
  1. Adoption—Religious aspects—Christianity. 2. Adoption—United
States. 3. Adoptees—Pastoral counseling—United States.
4. Adoptees—United States—Psychology. I. Title. II. Series.
HV875.26.N93   1999
362.73'4'0973—dc21   99-26278

For the adoptees of Colorado
who taught me that I did not know about
relinquishment and adoption

Contents

Foreword

The "primal wound" of relinquishment? "Ghost" parents? "Split-life" experience? Grief over being "given up"? Fantasies about birth parents providing a magical rescue mission? These are only some of the concepts to which I was introduced in this book. I had never seriously considered how the world of the adopted person is different. For example, adopted children draw upon two sets of parents for the "roots" which form their sense of self, and one of these sets is known only through the child's fantasy. How confusing can it be to come from two families when establishing one's identity?

Reading Ron's manuscript expanded my awareness of the experience of family, friends, and colleagues going through the search for their birth families and raising adopted children. Like buying another car and then noticing how many of the same make and model are on the road, it seemed that every week I encountered a person with an adoption story. If 2 percent of the American population is adopted, and you add four parents (two birth parents and two adopting parents) then about 10 percent of the population is involved with adoption. Understanding their experience is one of Ron's gifts to pastoral caregivers. I awaited each chapter eagerly to learn more about these dynamics.

My father lived with his family of origin until he was four years old, at which time his father was killed by a horse. He was adopted by a childless couple who were friends of his family, but by agreement never saw his family again. I have wondered how the trauma of this relinquishment and loss of family contributed to his struggles, particularly the search for affirmation and the difficulty with appropriate intimacy. As I read each of these chapters my insight about his life deepened.

What impact does relinquishment and adoption have on a child? Many move ahead with seeming ease, but as many as one-third of the adolescents in clinical treatment facilities are adopted. Think about the additional effect of relinquishment and adoption on the formation of basic trust, the perception of your place in the family constellation, self-acceptance, and the ability to take risks in relationships. Ron's familiarity with current psychological research on adoptees, plus his use of the work on early development by David Stern, the attachment theory of John Bowlby, the object-relations theory of D.W. Winnicott, the self psychology of Heinz

Kohut, the "Ghost Kingdom" of Betty Jean Lifton, Nancy Verrier's exploration of the "primal wound" of relinquishment, and the theology of hope of William Lynch, all inform his ability to help us make sense out of the unique dynamics of relinquishment and adoption.

In the last three chapters, Ron explores the place of hope, God-images, the "courage to be," and belonging in the relinquished and adopted person's life experience. In these pages the pastoral caregiver will find practical guidance in creatively applying these concepts in counseling with adoptees of all ages. You will find ways to help adoptees think through the spiritual and theological implications of their unique experience. His clinical vignettes constantly bring these concepts to life.

Ron writes as an advocate for the civil rights of adult adoptees who are seeking to learn about their birth parents. He points out that the shame-based culture of yesteryear led to a closed legal system that denies the rights of adoptees to know their history. Prophetically, he challenges the injustice of hiding important information about medical, ethnic, and psychological knowledge. He believes that knowing the whole story is vital to spiritual wellbeing.

The Counseling and Pastoral Theology Series

The purpose of this series is to address clinical issues that arise among particular populations currently neglected in the literature on pastoral care and counseling (women in lesbian relationships, African-American couples, adolescents under stress, women who are depressed, survivors of sexual abuse, adult adoptees, persons with terminal illness, and couples experiencing infertility). This series is committed to enhance both the theoretical base and the clinical expertise of pastoral caregivers by providing a pastoral theological paradigm that will inform both assessment and intervention with persons in these specific populations.

Many books on pastoral care and counseling are more carefully informed by the behavioral and social sciences than by classical theological disciplines. Pastoral care and counseling specialists have been criticized for ignoring our theological heritage, challenged to reevaluate our idolization of psychology, and to claim our unique perspectives on the human predicament. The discipline of pastoral theology has made significant strides in the last decade. The Society for Pastoral Theology was formed in 1985 and now publishes the *Journal of Pastoral Theology*.

Pastoral theology grows out of data gathered from at least three sources: 1) revelation about the human condition uncovered by the social and behavioral sciences, 2) wisdom from the classical theological disciplines, and 3) insight garnered from reflection on the pastoral ministry event. The development of pastoral theology grows out of the dialogue between these three perspectives, each perspective enabled to ask questions of, challenge, and critique the other perspectives.

Each author is clinically experienced and academically prepared to write about the particular population with which she or he is personally concerned and professionally involved. Each author develops a "constructive pastoral theology," developing the theological frame of reference that provides the unique perspective from which a pastoral person approaches both assessment and intervention. This constructive pastoral theology will enable clinically trained pastors and pastoral care specialists (pastoral counselors, chaplains, and CPE supervisors) to participate creatively in pastoral relationships that effectively enable healing, sustaining, guiding, reconciling, and liberating.

Though the focus will be on offering pastoral care and counseling to individuals, couples, and families, each author is cognizant of the interaction between individuals and their environment. These books will consider the effects of larger systems from family of origin to cultural constructs. Each author will use case material from her or his clinical pastoral ministry to focus the reader's attention on the issues faced by the particular population as viewed from the pastoral theological paradigm.

My thanks to colleagues who faithfully served on the Advisory Committee and expended many hours of creative work to ensure that this series would make a substantial contribution: Bonnie Miller-McLemore (1992–1996), Nancy Ramsay (1992–1996), Han van den Blink (1992–1994), Larry Graham (1994–1996), Linda Kirkland-Harris (1994–1996).

Andrew D. Lester
Brite Divinity School

Acknowledgments

If writing a book is like having a baby, then obviously more than one person is involved in the project. The idea may be there for years but unless something happens, nothing happens. Some good people made this happen. Thanks, first of all, to the adoptees who made me wonderfully curious about heartbeats that I could not understand. They were sitting on my shoulder the whole time it took to write this book. They are members of a Denver support group, Adoptees In Search, who were brave enough to make their voices known to a stranger. They explained themselves by word and deed in most eloquent ways, enough times so that I could understand. In their number are Beth Paddock, Richard Uhrlaub, Kathleen Odorizzi (a birth mother), Nancy O'Dair, Connie Dyk, Suzanne Matson, Elizabeth K. Traver, and Leslie Burget. This book is for them; yet they really wrote the book.

And then the midwives. Linda Olsen took the text to task to make it reader friendly. She helped me, corrected me, and taught me. The later chapters went better when I started to catch on to her care in the ways of saying things. Dave DeRidder helped with technical computer know-how whenever I needed him. Andy Lester patiently encouraged me along the way. And Chris Schlauch gave me the gift of his time and his brilliance in terms of teaching me to appreciate the many nuances of an idea. His remarkable ability to clarify theory and share his thoughts about the nature of human beings is only partially reflected in the book. He patiently helped me to see the many places where less than careful thinking rips away at the fabric of a good book. He made me want to learn. And, also, a word of appreciation to Catherine Carpenter and Nick Street of Westminster John Knox Press who helped in nursing the book along to life.

And a word of thanks to my wife, Sugar, who gave me away to this project for the many days of writing. Her care and support were there in Denver—seventy-five miles away from our cabin in the mountains where I sat pensively in the pine trees, working on the birth of this book. I promised Patches, our gray, Benjy-like terrier, that I would finish this book before he died an old-dog age. He would lie quietly, curled around my feet, as I sat restlessly by a six-hundred-hour candle, hoping for inspiration. I didn't keep the promise, but I'm thankful for a good friend who now lies buried in the pines. Finally, thanks to Dave Cady, Glenn Dykstra, and Henk Dykhouse, my fishing buddies. Conversations on Yellowstone Lake about the lives of our children stirred the wish that the next generation of boys and girls would grow up happy, maybe teasing cutthroat trout. Family and friends can make the challenges of life go easier. That truth is in the heart of this newborn book.

Adoptees Come of Age

Introduction: The Adoptee's Story

I hate my relinquishment; I love my adoption!

—*Elizabeth Starr*

I didn't know that I didn't know. Yes, I was a trained pastoral counselor with ten years of experience working with couples who came for help with their marriages. This couple seemed usual in its complaints—lack of intimacy, poor communication, and a nagging jealousy on the wife's part because her husband was spending so much time with his thirty-four-year-old secretary. It sounded like the typical scenario that middle-age couples present when, after twenty years of marriage, things unravel because of long-buried resentments that remain unresolved. So we went to work in conjoint and individual sessions of pastoral counseling, focusing on the dynamics of the relationship and the individual stories that created both connection and conflict for this couple. Three months later, little had changed. All of my "wonderful" suggestions to them had effected little change in their perceptions of each other. An exploration of their family histories and their current conflict fared no better. She was still resentful and jealous. He still liked his secretary.

Early in counseling Tom commented that he was adopted at infancy by parents who loved him and brought him up "pretty happy." I remember asking him how he felt about being adopted, wondering what meaning this had for him. He responded that for him it was "no big deal." He sounded convincing. I believed him. That was when our quiet collusion began.

Only after three months of marital counseling that seemingly went nowhere did I ask again about adoption. I sensed that somewhere something was missing, that an unspoken story needed to be told. This time I asked that he bring his adoption papers for review. (I had never seen any such documents and found myself curious about them.) He agreed and the following week he returned with a forty-one-year-old yellowed envelope that he had not examined "for years." He took out the decree of adoption and read it without reaction. Among other things it stated that he, at birth, had been "abandoned to the world." He came upon a description of his birth mother and handed it to me. I read it aloud. She was thirty-four years old at the time of his birth. She was tall with dark hair and brown eyes. Sensing a connection I asked about his secretary. His obsession with her had continued throughout the counseling. She *too* was tall with dark hair and brown eyes. When I suggested to Tom that perhaps he wanted to return to his birth mother/secretary, awareness dawned and this forty-two-year-old man wept deeply and *in a child's voice* wondered, "Why didn't she love me?"

Here began my education in the dynamics of relinquishment and adoption. In my own ignorance I had stumbled upon something that surprised and confused me. As a pastoral counselor, I was uninformed about relinquishment and adoption. Although "clinically trained," I, like the American culture of which I am a part, did not understand that relinquishment (the primal wound that may even be prenatal) and adoption (the early introduction to nonbiological parents) could have such a profound effect on the development of a person. I slowly learned that Tom had never grieved his relinquishment, which had occurred forty-two years ago at the Chicago Children's Aid and Home Society. He was two weeks old when his birth mother gave him to other parents. And, in his life, he had stretched as far as he could without grieving until he could no longer walk forward in life. At age forty-two his grief about the "primal wound"[1] of relinquishment was *in front* of him. He himself had been puzzled by the fact that he wished to be with his thirty-four-year-old secretary, but had no real romantic or sexual design in his mind for this relationship.[2] Her presence in his life was stimulating and fulfilling, but up to this moment in counseling he did not know why this might be. Now, with this dawning of understanding, the grief about his relinquishment flowed out of him like a river of sorrow. Together we discovered a source for some of his personal difficulties.

We discovered that his trouble wasn't really the marriage—it was Tom's inability to go on without resolving the pain of his relinquishment. It is important to note that it wasn't the adoption either. Although, during his development, there may have been some compromise in terms of his capacity for closeness, it was clear that he and his adoptive parents got along well, even up to the present time.

Relinquishment and adoption are two separate ongoing processes, not simply single separate events. Both have lifelong implications for adoptive development. This man, who married at age twenty, had inevitably set things up to play out the drama of his primal loss on the stage of his marriage. Needing to find a way to work through the pain of relinquishment, he recreated the players of his story of origin and found a way *back* to his unresolved grief.

After several months of significant depression the heaviness of the loss began to lift and he searched for, found, and met his birth mother. They have begun to develop a cordial relationship with an occasional phone call or letter. Tom's compulsive need to be with his secretary has subsided and, at the close of pastoral counseling, he reported more comfort within the boundaries of his own marriage. Although he still struggles to "be there" with his wife, there is movement in that direction. Grieving is difficult.

Looking back over ten years of pastoral counseling, I began to note what were probably missed opportunities for effective ministry because I didn't know about the impact of relinquishment and adoption. For adoptees, compromised attachments to people in many forms may be related to unfinished grieving and struggles with identity and closeness. Adopted persons *must* face these special problems in their development. To overlook the question of a counselee's story of relinquishment and adoption is to neglect to bring into focus a lived experience. Honoring that experience may be useful in effecting change and in bringing new direction to a person's life.

The purpose for this book is to acquaint the parish pastor and pastoral counselor and all three members of the adoption triad—adoptee, birth parent, adoptive parent—with some of the psychological and spiritual struggles that adopted persons may face in their development and in their adult life *because they are adoptees.* This book avoids pathologizing the plight of the adopted person and, instead, maps out an alternative, relatively normal developmental pathway that adoptees travel, given the realities of relinquishment and adoption. Children of adoption may grow up well, but they do grow up differently. These boys and girls, in contrast to their families-by-birth peers, are called on to navigate some troubled waters.

First, imagine what it is like to make sense of the idea of adoption as a three-, four-, or five-year-old child. It must be bewildering to think about being "in another mommy's tummy." Before children can conceptualize—usually around age six or seven—such a picture of origins is difficult, if not impossible, to understand. Life has begun in a puzzling way. Once awareness dawns, usually in latency (ages seven through ten), there may be a time of mourning, when the loss of real but "ghost" parents (a concept first developed by Betty Jean Lifton)[3] produces its first tears. Cognitive recognition of reality produces emotional pain. The impact of relinquishment will begin to strike home.

A second major issue for adoptees is their identity. Although all along in the first years of life there may be a struggle with identity as an adoptee, it is especially during adolescence that identity formation comes to the fore. Making sense of all the who-I-am pieces becomes a difficult developmental task. It is interesting to note that, although only 2 percent of the Western world population is composed of adopted persons, as many as one-third of adolescents in clinical treatment centers are adopted.[4] The over-representation of adoptees is significant. There may be a variety of reasons for this phenomenon, including the resources available to adoptive parents to seek help. Nevertheless, it probably indicates that something important is going on for adoptees during adolescence, something exceedingly difficult. Whatever problem this may be, it seems to subside in adulthood. Surveys of adult clinical populations show 2 percent of adopted adults in treatment.[5] So identity formation, which, of course, has lifelong implications for the sense of self that one develops, may be a major developmental challenge for an adoptee.

A third issue that adoptees may face with unusual difficulty is capacity for sustained intimacy. Although adoptees certainly do not have the corner on problems with closeness, there are some unusual reefs to navigate in terms of finding and keeping connection. Just as Tom, whom we met at the beginning of this chapter, described himself as drifting away from his wife, many adopted adults report that they struggle in relationships. They may marry—for security—someone who would never abandon them, and then find themselves horribly bored. Or they may form relationships that guarantee rejection—they will be relinquished in a replication of their primal wound. And, in between these two extremes, adoptees may find themselves in many relational configurations that are organized around unresolved difficulties with the dual processes of relinquishment and adoption. With regard to relationships, there is much at stake for children, adolescents, and adults of adoption.

A fourth challenge that adoptees face is the management of fantasies about birth parents and the possible resolution of these fantasies into reality by searching and reuniting with birth parents. Adoptees often report a rich fantasy life about their real but "ghost" birth parents. These stories are seldom told because many adoptees believe "they were not supposed to think about them." Nevertheless, adoptees often live between fantasy and reality in a way that can cause difficulties in knowing where the boundaries are on the inside or the outside. For some adoptees the difficulties of unresolved fantasies, in which parts of the adoptee self are not affirmed, make it difficult to "feel real," to be fully a person.[6] Birth parent fantasies that stay in place, unchanged and seemingly timeless over years or even decades, mean unanswered questions and unfinished identity formation. In search and reunion, to the degree that fantasy is exchanged and resolved into reality, adoptees have the opportunity to complete their identities, grieve, and develop a firmer grip on reality. This is an area of adoptive development only recently being explored.

One reason for writing this book is to emphasize the importance of effective pastoral care and counseling for adoptees who seek help. All too often, when childless couples adopt the babies of single mothers and absent fathers, we counselors find ourselves wanting to minimize the struggle of the birth mother and assist her to "get on with her life." We also want to support the adoptive family by giving our unqualified blessing to adoption and by raising no troubling issues. Unknowingly, we may participate in hiding the ongoing, sometimes lifelong, grieving of birth parents (more birth mothers, in number and intensity, than birth fathers). We bless the idea that love from adoptive parents is *enough* to bring adopted children along to maturity, as if the experience of relinquishment does not matter. It matters.

Effective pastoral counseling, which hopes to change perceptions of self and others and God, must be based on a growing understanding of all the dynamics, which collectively might be called the "secret side" of adoptive development. These dynamics have to do with the unasked-about and untold stories of the adoptee's struggles with sadness, with self-definition, and with ongoing closeness. They have to do with adoptees' fantasies of rescue by the real but "ghost" birth parents who are to magically solve the adopted child's problem with its adoptive family, if only they would show up. This part of the adopted person, living and growing under the lingering shadows of relinquishment, needs to be appreciated and honored by the pastoral counselor in order for transformation of that person to occur.

Another motivation for writing this book has to do with the social context and the legal precedents that surround relinquishment and adoption. Although the values and legal decisions of the past certainly included concern for adoptees, those shame-based decisions mean compromised legal and civil rights for adoptees today. We need to think about change with regard to relinquishment and adoption, change at a societal level, as a matter of not only increased emotional health and spiritual well-being but also of justice for adoptees. Pastoral theologian Larry Graham reminds us that "psyches create systems and systems create psyches"[7] and that ministry to only the individual psyche or soul of a person fails to encompass a needed ministry to the environment that shapes the person. This is especially true with relinquishment and adoption. Simply responding to the needs of the individual adoptee is not enough to effect the needed change in societal attitudes and the legal structures that hold the adoptee captive. For example, some adoptees choose to fight for years against the closed adoption system to search for their original birth certificates and the people whose names are on them. Liberation and full adult status for adoptees in our society will entail critical rethinking of how values and laws have determined negative meaning and not-so-subtle limitations in their lives. And so, adequate pastoral care must encompass not only the struggles of the individual but also the problems of societal structures.

Imagine what it's like, time and again, to be told in a variety of ways that birth parents and birth history, the stories of one's beginnings, don't matter. Consider what it's like to be a twelve-year-old adopted boy who can never know whether his birth mother or birth father is all right, especially if he thinks about them often. Or, wonder, for a moment, what it's like for a forty-nine-year-old adopted woman to stand in line with adolescents before a *juvenile* court judge, seeking information in *closed* adoption records which could lead to further connection to an elderly birth mother whom she would like to meet before that birth mother dies. And what about the injustice of withholding important medical information about potentially life-threatening diseases from adoptees because of closed adoption records? There are as many as four thousand genetically related physical diseases.

Adoptees are often at a social disadvantage, reporting that they feel discriminated against by societal attitudes about adoption and by a closed legal system that denies them access to their own complete identity and the status of adulthood. These things mean that it is *more* difficult to grow up adopted in our society today. Certainly, the rights of adoptees need to be held in balance with the rights of birth parents and adoptive parents. But many adoptees see themselves as persons without a voice in relinquishment or in adoptive decisions about which they want to know more. The cry of the adoptee in our society is not simply a complaint about emotional and spiritual suffering, it is also a demand for fairness in the courtroom—for the civil and human right to know one's own historical identity.

A word about resilience. An adopted child must navigate a unique, sometimes complicated development. It may be difficult, but in comparison to what? Some relinquished and adopted persons grow up very well without consciously dealing with the issues that this book raises. And nonadopted peers may, for other reasons, grow up with greater difficulty than adoptees. The tasks of development are unique to each of us to some degree. The resilience that some children demonstrate when facing challenges like relinquishment is always of interest. Despite the comparisons made in this book between adoptees in general and their nonadopted peers in general, we must remember that these generalizations are limited by the many wonderful ways the human mind creates to manage difficulty. Adoptees may hurt in unusual ways, but they do not have the corner on human suffering. They tell us, if we can listen well, of just one of the many human journeys in between joy and sadness. It is a road that simply deserves to be honored as a legitimate path for people once called "illegitimate."

And also a word about the limits of this book. Strictly speaking, *Adoptees Come of Age* is only about the adoptee's experience of relinquishment, of having been let go by "ghost parents." It is not about adoption, if by this term we refer strictly to the relationships between adoptees and their adoptive families. The specific struggles that adoptees may have with these attachments are discussed only in a secondary fashion as they both assist and hamper the adoptees' struggles with their birth parents, the "ghost parents" of their quiet longings and secret fantasies. The dynamics that are common in adoptive families where relinquished and adopted children *do* their work with grieving and identity and intimacy and fantasy are important factors in terms of influencing development. But they lie beyond the reach of this book. In this text we will listen for the heartbeat of adoptees as they relate to the parents who gave them history and genetic lines and birth.

The Plan of the Book

In chapter 1 we see the adoptee as a person who faces unusual challenges, perhaps the foremost being the impact of relinquishment on the adoptee's emotional and spiritual development from childhood all the way to adulthood. Relinquishment and adoption are two separate, parallel processes (not simply events) that influence and impact each other throughout the adoptee's life. As adoptees seek wholeness in adult life, they must manage a "split-life experience"[8] at several levels. Every day in some way they must manage the "twoness" of being part of two different families. Adoptees must also deal with societal attitudes and beliefs about relinquishment and adoption which tend to deny who they really are as adopted persons. For the past fifty years, adoptive laws and practices have put adoptees at a disadvantage by hiding their complete identities and disallowing their feelings of grief and bewilderment about relinquishment. The recent press for more openness in adoption brings hope of improving this situation, but there remains a long legacy of denial and disadvantage for today's adoptees. Growing up with "ghost parents" is difficult in many ways. Chapter 1 will explain this challenge and offer a new perspective on the adoptee as a person, helping adoptees to understand and to define themselves more clearly.

The adoptive family is formed out of loss. Adopted children must weather the storm of being placed with new parents who learn slowly and sometimes awkwardly who their adopted children are and how they manage life. This exchange of parents is a real and profound loss, but research today is less than clear about how deep a wound it may be. Whether there is prenatal grief and grief at birth concerning relinquishment is debated. Some believe "the primal wound" of relinquishment has lifelong impact on development. Further along in development, when the cognitive capacity to conceptualize is achieved, another wave of grieving often sweeps over adopted children. This occurs when they finally understand that there are real "ghost parents" out there who mean something to them. Chapter 2 treats this grieving of relinquishment as natural and necessary in adoptive experience.

The identity of the adoptee is complicated by the fact that children of adoption grow up in what has been called a "double representational world."[9] This means that during development a relinquished and adopted child draws upon *two* sets of parents for internalizations that form the sense of self. Both genetics and environment play significant roles in contributing pieces of identity to the puzzle of the person. Chapter 3 explores these primitive components of a basic sense of self, drawing upon the work of Daniel Stern in terms of his discussion of the self of the human infant. We see how hope for an ongoing connection to birth parents is an intrinsic part of identity formation and examine the developmental struggles of children who are literally looking for themselves in the mirror as much as in the family picture. The rekindling of identity concerns that is common to adolescence is presented in the context of the significant overrepresentation of adolescent adoptees in clinical populations. Issues of identity in adulthood are presented in relation to the relatively new phenomenon of searching for birth parents. This sets the stage for a discussion of other struggles, once the self of the adoptee is relatively in place.

Given the developmental difficulties that adoptees face in terms of grieving and identity formation, it's no wonder that, for adoptees, love and marriage are sometimes complicated by a compromised capacity to connect—the topic of chapter 4. Sustained intimacy demands a basic trust in people. This, of course, relates directly not only to marital relationships but also to family connections and friendships in general. However, because the pain of the abandonment hangs in the background of adoptive life, fear sometimes comes to the fore in these relationships. Roadblocks to intimacy that characterize the experience of many adoptees are presented, along psychodynamic lines, in terms of defense and repetition compulsion. Drawing on the attachment theory of John Bowlby, chapter 4 relates the struggles that adoptees sometimes report having with closeness to difficulties that they may have with both sets of parents. Special attention is paid to the romantic choices that adoptees sometimes make. This chapter concludes with a story of love which demonstrates how deeply the power of attraction can relate directly to unresolved pain around the wound of relinquishment.

Chapter 5 explores the emotional dimensions of an adoptee's life through the unusual fantasy lives of adoptees. In the adopted person's intersubjective world, where play, illusion, and imagination are central to forming both self-perceptions and relations with others, birth parents hold a special place. Based on the object-relations theory of Donald Woods Winnicott, a psychological perspective is developed by which to view the experience of adoptees as people who sometimes struggle to maintain these important connections in their lives. Although most adopted persons report a rich fantasy experience from childhood on, seldom do others ask them about such things. Interviews with adoptees searching for reunion with birth parents show that forming fantasies about their birth parents kept them "psychically alive" in important ways.

One of the guiding spiritual forces that presses adoptees forward toward their future is a sense of hopefulness. Hope drives development, especially for adoptees who struggle to complete their personal identities and know themselves fully. Chapter 6 presents hope as a spiritual lens through which to explore the experience of adopted persons. Keeping hope alive, as well as guarding *against* being too hopeful, is the spiritual path of many adoptees. For many, it is an open question how present God is in their lives, given their experience of early abandonment and ongoing societal discrimination. The wonderful idea of a loving, caring God is sometimes seen in sharp contrast to beginning their lives "up for grabs," supposedly unwanted, and unsure about strange surroundings and new people, *regardless* of how caring their adoptive parents might be. A theology of hope is presented, based in part on the "images of hope" described by Father William F. Lynch in his book by that name. Hope will be used as a theological construct to explain how adopted persons experience their lives.

Chapter 7 considers faith development in terms of the God representations that are formed in early childhood, perhaps from the earliest interactions with the parents. When the primal connection of attachment to a birth mother is broken, adoptees can be at risk in terms of the capacity for faith in God as a loving, benevolent presence in their lives. Fantasies of birth parents may be negative and uninviting. The writings of Ana-Maria Rizzuto raise the issue of correlations and connections between parental images and God representations. From Heinz Kohut we get another perspective on the idea of God as a primitive and important idealization that strengthens the emerging self by giving a child a vital connection to a source of strength and permanence. Tillich's notion of the "courage to be" is reviewed in terms of the spiritual experience of adoptees as they deal with the "nonbeing" of relinquishment. This chapter concludes with ideas for development of faith for adoptees in terms of the hope of reexperiencing God in a new way, a special challenge for the community of faith.

Chapter 8 concludes the book with a personal reflection on the idea of belonging as a theme of ministry. Pastoral counselors dealing with relinquishment and adoption need a dual focus on *both* sets of parents in terms of belonging. Belonging is explored by way of the ideas of being claimed, being understood, being appreciated, and being protected. We also look at ethical concerns that surround the issues involved in relinquishment in American society. The shame-based decision making of fifty years ago has blinded our society to the importance of the basic human Christian values of responsibility for actions, truth, justice, human dignity, and reconciliation. The book concludes with a reflection on the importance of the restoration of the humanity of adoptees and nonadoptees alike!

Chapter One

Hearing a Dissonant Echo:
The Adoptee as a Person

I have two sets of parents, one set inside of me, and one set outside of me.
—*Sarah, a fifteen-year-old adoptee*

Imagine pitching a rock into a deep granite canyon, anticipating the clatter of resounding echos as it descends to the canyon floor . . . and then hearing another echo from a different place as if another rock had also been thrown. How unexpected and disconcerting! How might somone make sense of that experience? Did I really hear that other echo when my rock hit the canyon floor? I might question my reality, second guessing whether I really heard the sound. After all I was alone. No one else was there to throw a rock. Or perhaps I would acknowledge the dissonant echo but immediately dismiss it as a sound unrelated to my rock throwing. But what if somehow these echos were related in a way that I could not understand? What if magically in the midair of personal inquiry the one rock became two, both of which set off an antiphony of echos? The adoptee who has ears to hear—and most do—will pick up the dissonant echo, a clue to the deep mysteries that surround relinquishment and adoption.

Adoptees can grow up well, but they grow up differently. They must inevitably follow an unusual developmental pathway as they attend to the sound of that dissonant echo. They are challenged to face unique dilemmas that influence the very nature of their relationships to themselves, to the many people in their lives, and, in an ultimate sense, to God. They start life in an unusual way, and though at times it may be faint, they hear another echo in their personal stories which makes them unique as persons. It's all fascinating.

Carl, age eleven, came to my office for pastoral counseling because he was having difficulty with some of his relationships at school. The schoolyard bully regularly picked on Carl, and despite his relatively large size, Carl just would not fight back. His grades had dropped and he reported that schoolwork was "boring." He was unmotivated about doing homework. In general Carl was a depressed young boy. In contrast to many clinical situations when the counselee has little idea about the possible reasons for feeling blue, Carl said he knew exactly why he was so sad. It was because of Patty, his birth mother. Carl was worried about her. He wanted to know whether she was OK. He hoped he would hear from her "one of these days." Carl's adoption was semi-open, meaning that an adoption agency keeps confidential all identifying information such as last names, addresses, and phone numbers. Therefore, Carl's adoptive parents and Patty could correspond indirectly through the adoption agency that placed him. When Carl was five years old, Patty had paid a visit to see him at the agency office. Carl had some memory of that visit and wanted to see her again.

Carl's relationship with his adoptive parents appeared to be good. His parents were unusual in their openness to Carl's longing to know more about Patty. His adoptive father was soft-spoken and consistently empathic to his son's difficulties. His adoptive mother was more forceful at times. Carl complained that she yelled at him too much. She was aware of this, open about it, and attributed some of her behavior to the importance of being a good mother, especially because of her own disappointments with infertility. She was not defensive in dealing with this struggle. She really wanted to help Carl, to let him cry in her arms about the "Patty pain." But Carl struggled with letting either parent share his suffering. He said he needed Patty.

Arrangements were made through the agency for correspondence to begin between Carl and Patty. This idea encouraged Carl. His mood improved and his grades went up. A sense of calm returned to this adoptive family. The clinical responses to Carl's birth mother echo were sufficient, at least for the time being.

The Suitcase

As with all his relinquished peers, Carl brought along an important suitcase to his adoptive home. This luggage of childhood for many adoptees is filled with both wonderful treasures and heavy stones. The treasures that are precious include things like dominant genes for rich auburn hair or great musical talent. There may be inherited abilities to be artistic or athletic or handsome or blessed with long dark eyelashes. Other treasures in this suitcase may be early memories or fantasies of care from birth parents. Depending on the age at which a child is adopted, the form of such connections will of course vary, but the treasures, like the gift of a teddy bear, are the remembered or fantasized connections. These carry special value in adoptive childhood.

There are also heavy stones in the suitcase. The rejection that necessarily comes with relinquishment, being surrendered to nonbiological adoptive parents, is usually a big stone to carry. Some of the stones are questions about the why of relinquishment or the whereabouts of the birth parents. Other stones may be fears of medical dangers such as a birth family history of breast cancer or another genetically related disease. Another stone may be shame about an accidental conception between partners who left each other in the secrecy of nighttime instead of staying together in the daytime of marital love. Or it may be shame that you were not good enough or important enough to be kept, to be claimed, or to be parented by the people who created you. Any of these painful realities can make the suitcase heavy. This was true for Carl on the day that he came to see me. Other adopted children are hardly aware that this emotional and spiritual luggage is there. It sits in the closet unnoticed until someone tries to move it. Then its weight becomes apparent.

These precious treasures and heavy stones are all realities that accompany relinquishment and become some of the components for a sense of self, in either a positive or negative way. Sometimes they become the missing pieces of an adoptee's personal story, missing because the suitcase either stays shut, is opened in secret, or is peeked into occasionally and then closed because it feels painful or because a child is told not to bother opening it in the light of adoptive development. Yes, adoptees can grow up well, but there's baggage to which they must attend.

Relinquishment and Adoption Are Different

When Carl came to my office, he was certainly carrying his suitcase. And it was so heavy that he needed both hands on the handle to pull it into the room. There were both memories and fantasies about Patty as well as lingering questions about her care for Carl. How hard or how easy was it for Patty to relinquish him? Did she think about him much? Was she really OK? What would it be like for him to be living with *her* now? Would she treat him well, better than his adoptive parents? Should he be jealous of his half brother who had not been relinquished and who was now living with her?

Carl had answers to none of these questions, but the questions were never far from his consciousness as he managed daily life in his adoptive family. The point, first of all, is that these thoughts and the possibly painful feelings that accompanied them challenged Carl in his development. Carl was very aware of the difficulty of dealing with the *twoness* of being a relinquished and adopted person. On the one hand, Carl's developmental task was to attach to his adoptive parents so that his emotional and spiritual growth could occur. But, on the other hand, and perhaps more quietly, Carl needed to attend to the feelings that stayed in his awareness day after day about his *ongoing connection* to Patty. This truly is the conflict of the relinquished and adopted person. Adoptees are always members of both their birth and adoptive families. In different ways, they live within each. How does one do *both* and do them both well? It may be very difficult.

There are issues to deal with on both sides of this developmental fence. As the relinquished and adopted child grows up, this experience of twoness is always present in some way. Carl often refused care from his adoptive parents because it made him feel somehow disloyal to Patty. He lived in between two sets of parents. Sometimes this twoness got to him. But Carl's dilemma was and is further complicated by the unfortunate way in which relinquishment and adoption have been gathered together in the word "adoption." This is not simply a matter of semantics. In our very language, as a culture, we reveal our societal denial of the difference between relinquishment and adoption. One of the most important distinctions that this book will present, and one that society has largely neglected, is the difference between relinquishment and adoption.

One thoughtful, articulate adopted woman said it this way: "I hate my relinquishment; I love my adoption!" Relinquishment and adoption have been carelessly combined in our speech as if to refer to a single moment in time when an infant or child is legally placed with new, nonbiological parents. This is an unhelpful muddling of thinking which has significant negative consequences in terms of how people understand the challenges of adoptive development. The fact is that *relinquishment and adoption are separate, although parallel, lifelong processes that influence and impact each other in a variety of ways*. It is an important distinction. The two things are experienced separately. They are experienced ambivalently, loaded, as we shall see, with lots of emotional meaning. And they are experienced as interacting with each other, informing and challenging the way adoptees understand their histories, their identities, and their hearts.

Relinquishment, first of all, is both a historical event and a lifelong process in the adoptive experience. The event is the legal decision by the birth parents to give up parental rights to a child and possibly make plans for adoption. This moment in a relinquished person's history may be powerful and painful and may mark a real injury in terms of the early development of the self. But relinquishment is also a process in several ways. As the days and years go by, the relinquished child may quietly wonder about, be sad about the loss of the real but "ghost" birth parents, those people who exist both in reality and in fantasy for adopted children. Well, it always hurts to grieve. It may take years of openness and mourning for people like Carl to truly come to terms with the pain of rejection triggered by relinquishment. In adolescence, the process of relinquishment continues as adopted young people struggle to carve out their identities from the kaleidoscope of personal parts that having four parents entails. So relinquishment, being released from birth parents, continues as a separate issue of concern as adoptees grow up.

But there's more. Young adults as well as older adults who were relinquished may enter relationships with great ambivalence. In the face of the pain of the primal wound of relinquishment, they may create relationships that guarantee safety—the security of knowing that rejection will not occur a second time. These relationships, which are organized for bullet-proof security, may mean immense dependency or intense control on the part of the adoptee; either way they are designed so that rejection will not reoccur. Or else adoptees may form relationships in such a way that they recreate the painful drama of rejection in the drama of divorce. The adoptee may (less than consciously) set things up so that he faces relinquishment once again by a mate that he has abused or pushed away. In any case *the reality of being relinquished, of losing one's birth parents, may serve as the guiding force by which one determines the shape of personal connections.* And then relinquishment, with its own painful power, goes on and on in adult life. Put differently, the echo of relinquishment may sound off the walls of the adoptee's canyon in times of crisis and personal pain.

Adoption is first of all a reference to the legal transaction by which parental rights are transferred to a nonbiological parent or parents. Adoption is both this initial event of bonding to the adoptive parent(s) and the lifelong process of attachment and detachment with adoptive parents in the formation of the adoptive family. Whereas relinquishment refers to the loss of parents, adoption refers to the gain of new parents. Adoption creates connections with a new mother, a new father, and possibly new siblings. These connections are critical parts of successful adoptive development because they serve as the basic sources of nurture and support for relinquished children. Just as any relationship with parents is a process, adoption is a life of ebb and flow of connection that keeps adopted children emotionally and spiritually alive while on their way to adulthood. The term "adoption" is best used to make reference only to these relationships. Adoption is a separate process—distinct from relinquishment—that relates to a person's role in an adoptive family.

Once this distinction between relinquishment and adoption becomes clear, the interface between them comes to light in a useful, liberating way. Relinquishment and adoption influence and impact each other in important ways, both positively and negatively. First of all, if relinquishment, particularly at a later age, is profoundly painful for children, they may disallow the connection of adoption, at least to some degree. For example, an adoptive mother recalls the first hours of adoption with her infant daughter, who screamed inconsolably for four hours after arriving at her new home. This particular protest against relinquishment was intense—in no way the adoptive mother's fault. In fact her daughter's protest was against both her relinquishment and her adoption. She wanted neither. For years this adoptive mother struggled for connection to her daughter, whose protest continued throughout childhood. In this story the unconsoled pain of relinquishment compromised the strength of the adoptive attachment. This interface becomes increasingly complicated because the connection of initial bonding and ongoing attachment serves as the fuel needed to *do* the necessary grieving that accompanies relinquishment. This is the first catch-22 dilemma for the adopted child in that *the very attachment needed for healthy development may be impacted by the injury of the primal wound of relinquishment.* Insufficient attachment may mean that an adopted child shuts down inside and defensively avoids getting the job of mourning done because, without sufficient connection, it hurts too much to (consciously) know the injury of rejection. Adoption, as a separate process, is the healing resource for the relinquished child just as parental care is the critical foundation for mental and spiritual health for the rest of us. In this sense, adoption is a critically important, wonderful thing for relinquished children.

Sorting out this distinction between relinquishment and adoption allows for new awareness and greater self-understanding for adopted people. It serves to help adoptees appreciate the many and confusing emotional responses that they have in the course of their development. Understanding how these separate, parallel processes function and interface with each other brings clarity to the psychic tasks of both grieving and attachment. However, when relinquishment and adoption are collapsed into one issue, as has been the case for the past several decades, the unusual difficulties that surround relinquishment remain shrouded in quiet mystery. And the adoptee pays the price.

The Split-Life Experience

Adoptees, out of necessity, live what Betty Jean Lifton, author, adoptee, and adoption reform advocate, calls a "split-life experience."[1] Their relinquishment and adoption force them to manage two separate realities, one a birth family reality and the other an adoptive family reality. This was not always thought to be so. From about 1940 to 1970, the period when adoption transactions were closed, many believed that the love of adoptive parents was *enough* to bring a relinquished and adopted child along to maturity. They believed that the adoptee could and should forget the past, the story of the birth parents, the reasons for relinquishment, the question of medical history—all the secret other side of adoptive development. Adoption professionals believed that not knowing was best for all three of the triad members. Until fairly recently it was thought that an adopted child did not need to grieve because birth parents could simply be forgotten. Or that an adoptee who was troubled by sadness about the relinquishment could just "get over" the grieving. Then the mending could occur that would allow the adoptee a fully integrated life experience. But not so.

Being a relinquished and adopted person means managing and accepting a dual identity that is part of an ongoing split-life experience. Researcher Paul Brinich suggests that the adopted child lives in a "double representational world,"[2] which means there are four mental representations or psychic pictures of parents: the birth parents and the adoptive parents. The adoptee draws on these pictures to make sense of his world and to develop his personal identity. Brinich describes how this developmental challenge is sometimes so difficult that the ego of the adoptee settles for splitting these objects, making one set of parents good and the other bad in order to save the psychic day. He describes how troublesome it is to remain honestly and usefully ambivalent about each of the four parents; seeing the strengths and weaknesses of each. For our purpose, he helps to describe the way in which each adoptee must manage the two realities of adoptive living: the split-life experience that may never be thoroughly resolved. The great temptation for both adoptees and adoptive parents is the denial of birth parents, the collapse of relinquishment into adoption, as if only adoption matters and as if only adoptive parents define reality for the adoptee. It's just not that way.

Accepting the nature of this dual reality is no easy task. Returning to Carl's story, we see that for some adopted children it feels impossible to accept this, even though it must be done at least to some degree. How shall we view Carl's dilemma with Patty, his birth mother? Should we as pastors or pastoral counselors, adoptive parents (and birth parents too), or friends of his family think that we help best if we help Carl "get over" his lingering connection to Patty? Ought we remind him by how we talk of this that he really *should* find a way to forget about her, to grieve enough that she does not matter anymore in his life? For nearly fifty years adoption professionals and the general public have thought so. Or would we be more pastoral if we believed and therefore suggested that Carl be given permission and encouraged to honor his birth parent connection to Patty because she is a real part of his real story? What is this echo he reports?

Quite obviously our belief, our clinical theory of adoptive personhood, will guide our responses. If as pastors and pastoral counselors we appropriate an understanding that the adoptee is indeed called upon to live a split-life experience, then we will respond in a particular way. If this dual reality experience is not to be mended or fixed, but instead honored and accepted, we will respond in a manner that reflects such belief and, quite empathically, assist the adoptee *out* of the impossible bind of trying to follow recent societal beliefs that, first, relinquishment does not matter, and, second, that healthy adoptees can indeed live a unified life in the single dimension of adoptive life. Neither is the case.

Most of us have two arms. We walk through life left-handed or right-handed or even ambidextrous, well aware that on *each* side of our bodies an arm is ready to do its work or play. But imagine the impact on a child growing up if only *one* arm was ever noticed or acknowledged, as if the other arm just did not exist. Imagine that mirroring parents commented, "What a strong arm you have!" or "How slender your arm *is*!" Understandably, the child would experience confusion and discomfort about herself and her body. She knows that she has two arms, and she would wonder, first, why the other arm is never mentioned or noticed and, eventually, whether that other arm is real. We need the validation of others to know our bodies and our selves. Adoptees need validation of their birth stories if they are to feel fully real. But adopted people sometimes experience life as one-armed people, though they know that the other arm, which points to their birth histories and birth parents, is there somewhere. They do have two arms and they do have two sets of parents and they do have two realities to honor as they grow toward maturity.

Relinquishment Sensitivity

Bringing the "arm" of relinquishment back into view and affirming it as part of an adoptee's story allows for new understandings for some of the struggles that adoptees report. One of the more interesting struggles might be called "relinquishment sensitivity." Barb, for example, is an adopted adult with a college degree in communications. After the early years of raising her two children she decided that, with both children in school, part-time employment would be a good idea for her. She prepared an up-to-date resumé listing her experience of coordinating volunteer services in school programs and in an adoptee support and advocacy organization. She has credentials, but she can barely bring herself to present her resumé or fill out a job application, much less personally interview for a position. She hesitates to take the first step. Why? Some adoptees know, some don't, but often the reason is simply the fear of being rejected *again*. It would hurt too much, so possibilities for rejection in every area of life are carefully avoided.

Relinquishment sensitivity has to do with a special sense of hurt that accompanies rejection in its many forms. It is a not-so-subtle sting triggered by life's disappointments that seems to have reverberations all the way to an adopted person's core beliefs about value as a person or rights as a citizen. This sensitivity may be disguised by anger or depression, but the underlying hurt, reminiscent of the primal wound of relinquishment, is the most basic factor. For example, when an adopted adolescent is sent away to a boarding school, there is often not only separation anxiety from adoptive parents but also (unspoken) anguish around feeling rejected, "put up" for parenting by someone else again—this time the boarding school teachers. And this understandably reinforces a negative self-image, a personal doubt about one's (compromised) value as one who should be kept. And the sting of rejection surfaces once again.

In the story of Carl we see this sensitivity. Carl, despite being sizable in relation to his peers, always refused to fight back, to push back against Jesse, the schoolyard bully. Something was locked up inside Carl that would not allow him to use his strong arms to defend himself. Carl reported feeling intensely angry when he saw Jesse picking on someone else in the school yard. Why all this intense anger without reaction? Carl seemed paralyzed about defending himself or another. Carl saw the school-yard abuse as rejection, whether of him or of his picked-on peers. He was able to acknowledge that facing Jesse meant facing the threat of rejection once again, and that "it would hurt too much." The hurt of being bullied was less painful than the sting of being openly rejected. He would not push back because he had to protect himself from experiencing a deeper pain, the pain of being rejected, which echoed to the core of his eleven-year-old being and to his beginning. For Carl, relinquishment mattered a lot. For whatever reason, Patty rejected him, and he worked hard to avoid any further rejection. Carl was relinquishment sensitive. So are many other children, adolescents, and adults who were relinquished when their lives began.

Societal Disadvantage

But Carl's story, as well as the stories of most adoptees, is not simply about the struggle on the inside in terms of emotional and spiritual concerns. It is also about the story on the outside in terms of the feelings, the thoughts, and the attitudes of others with regard to relinquishment and adoption. Adoptees must deal in some way with the messages they receive from a society that suggests that relinquishment does not matter. Relatives may look at them as if they are not quite part of the family. Teachers and school counselors may believe that it is best to forget what cannot be changed. So the adoptee is at a social disadvantage. Homes for unwed mothers (notice the stigma), for example, were the solution of choice for many from the 1940s into the 1970s. The disgrace of having a daughter who was pregnant outside of marriage was managed by sending the daughter off to another state for the birth and relinquishment. Thereafter she would be "returned" to (Anglo-American) society as if the pregnancy had never occurred. The Florence Critenton Home in Denver gave each pregnant woman a false name for the duration of her stay. Her true identity was kept secret to protect her from the shame of her iniquity. She would have been judged harshly and shamed by many, including family members, if her pregnancy were known. However, her relinquishment, the surrender of her child, was seen as her redemption. It led to her restoration to society and her escape from living at a societal disadvantage as an immoral woman with an illegitimate child. Given the historical context of the early decades of this century, relinquishment and adoption were looked upon as a caring choice to remedy the problems of societal disadvantage associated with the sin of nonmarital pregnancy. Relinquishment was thought to be a benevolent solution for everyone involved. The birth mother was offered "as if" status: as if never pregnant, that is. (Birth fathers were shadows in these stories, never openly addressed, hardly noticed within the double standard of blame.) The adoptive parents who received the surrendered child were given "as if" status, too: that is, parents as if by birth. The changed/falsified birth certificate made it so. And the adoptee was given "as if" status as well: as if by birth to nonbiological parents, *not* a "bastard" child. Adoptive status was meant to somehow erase the societal stigma of illegitimacy. So it was that forty to fifty years ago 95 percent of single, pregnant Anglo-American women "chose" to relinquish their children and then be saved from a societal disadvantage.

Yet today all three parties in that triad are disadvantaged after all. Although the shame-based decisions of fifty years ago may have been expressions of concern in some way for each of the parties involved, they unintentionally left a legacy of denial and secrecy which inevitably compromised complete identity and a full life for adoptees. Many birth mothers report that they have grieved unendingly about the pressured decision to surrender. Many adoptive parents live with an unfortunate stigma about infertility. But the birth mothers and adoptive parents face these difficulties as teenagers or adults. Adoptees must face relinquishment and adoption as children. They have no voice in these decisions, yet they must deal with the lifelong ramifications. One ramification is, unfortunately, to live at a societal disadvantage.

Len is fifty-seven years old, adopted fifty-six and a half years ago. After raising a family, surviving a difficult divorce, and struggling with an inability to make a commitment in a new relationship, he decided that it might be good for him to seek out some information about his birth story and his birth parents. He was curious. First, he petitioned the court of his adoption to open the file for his review. He spent several thousand dollars. However, because he had no "just cause" for opening the record, his request was quickly denied. A "just cause" is a legal reason that is sufficient to override the demand for confidentiality in the closed records system. Len next petitioned to the court to have his request processed through a state-sponsored intermediary program whereby confidential intermediaries locate and talk with birth parents, birth siblings, or birth children to determine whether the exchange of information or reunion would be acceptable to the "other" party involved. However, the local magistrate, who does not support the program, has refused to release Len's record to intermediaries, along with refusing nearly 350 other requests. Len waits and lives at a societal disadvantage under the guise of the law. The laws written years ago with honorable intent in terms of social escape from shame leave Len not knowing what he wants to know, but believing that he has a civil and human right to know. Who is he? Who are his birth parents? Being adopted means living under the cloud of discrimination.

Pat's story is somewhat different. A year ago, at age forty-one, she was given the diagnosis of multiple sclerosis. For several years she had troubling symptoms of the disease and so she proceeded with legal council to petition the court of her adoption to open her record based on the "just cause" of needing to know her medical history in order to assist the physicians in her care. Three thousand dollars later, her request was denied as lacking the substance of "just cause." Pat lives with a medical disadvantage that she considers discriminating, another form of societal disadvantage.

Wendy is a twenty-three-year-old adoptee who recently learned that two years ago her birth mother in Michigan, a thousand miles away, died of breast cancer. Before her death Wendy's birth mother requested that her birth daughter be informed. It took two years for the adoption agency involved to clear the way and find Wendy to give her this information. Wendy's mammogram proved negative, but the story could have turned out differently. Not only is it awkward to repeatedly announce in doctors' offices "no medical history, I'm adopted," it also puts adoptees at medical risk, another disadvantage.

In addition to legal disadvantage and medical disadvantage, there may also be societal disadvantage simply in terms of how adoptees are viewed. Not so long ago adopted people were considered "the product of bad seed"[3] because of assumptions about the birth parents involved—people who would do such things as having illicit sex. A cloud of shame covered the stories of relinquishment and adoption, which gave negative status to the adoptee. They were considered people of "not such good stock," as unworthy of social status, and lesser in value; certainly this was a social disadvantage.

Carol, for example, is one of nine adopted children of a couple who managed a farm in southern Montana. Adopted at age three, after heart surgery and two and a half years of foster care, she grew up in a community where adoption was common. Her memories were of living on a "plantation," as she called it, where the children did the farm chores and did them well, but without appreciation. She recalls the disdain of her peers, who in elementary school poked fun at adoptees there with comments like "no wonder your real parents did not want you." Such were the wounds of this "servant girl" as she grew up. In her experience, her adoptive parents, her peers at school, and society at large saw her as a "lesser human being" because she was adopted. This gave them license to exploit and emotionally abuse her in ways that made growing up especially painful. Our focus here, however, is not on her personal difficulties but on society's attitude years ago toward her because she was an adoptee. She grew up at a social disadvantage.

Never an Adult

The adoptee may feel that the status of adulthood is never quite within reach. In several ways to be an adoptee is to always be seen as a child. A twenty-nine-year-old adoptee was searching for her birth mother when she came upon what might be the name and phone number of her birth mother's sister, her aunt by birth. Jane mustered the courage to make the phone call, to be met by the great exclamation, "Honey! The baby is on the phone!" This twenty-nine-year-old adult was *still* the baby. Frozen in time, despite the years that had passed, this woman was in the memories and fantasies of the birth family as an infant. In their minds she had never grown up, and on the occasion of this moment of reunion she *felt* as if she had never grown up. As a relinquished adoptee, Jane experienced herself as an adult child, not a mature person in the eyes of others. She was still the baby.

But there's more to the story. Jane grew up as the oldest of three adopted children in a well-to-do family. She recalls that, when she was a child, whenever her family would travel, her adoptive mother would become extremely anxious in airports. Jane's mother would become hypervigilant, holding tightly to the hands of her children, fearful that someone would take them away. This frightened, overprotective mother may have been responding to her own feelings about her infertility and her fear that she would lose her children because she had "taken" them in the first place. "Taken" children could be taken again. Many adoptive parents report the fear of losing the children that they have received by adoption. Whatever the reasons, her adoptive mother's response to her had an infantilizing effect, for it told Jane that the world was a frightening place and she ought *not* venture too far out into it. This overprotection kept Jane a child. Her individuation was in spite of her mother rather than with her mother's help. Fear keeps children from feeling like adults.

When Jane began her search as a twenty-eight-year-old adult, she was treated by the legal system as a child. Like many other adoptees, she had to begin her search in *juvenile* court to request that her records be presented to a state-appointed confidential intermediary. She felt a childlike status in her legal battles. The law kept her a child. Her request that she be treated as an adult with rights to information about her medical history and personal identity is certainly a challenge to the legal system which, years ago, compromised her rights to such things. To give Jane adult status is to recognize her civil and human right to her history and her identity. Such recognition challenges many of the principles that guided decisions about relinquishment and adoption years ago. These legal codes change slowly. (Only three states—Kansas, Alaska, and Tennessee—have open records laws. At this writing the Tennessee law is being challenged in the state supreme court.) So, for Jane, the legal system always kept her juvenile.

Not only does Jane feel that society, her overprotective adoptive parents, and the legal system see her as a child, but Jane sees herself as little. Many adoptees find it difficult to see themselves as adult, as grown up, when grief about birth parent loss is unresolved or when pieces of the puzzle of identity are not in place. Unfortunately, adoptees can infantilize themselves in an understandable defense against inner pain. Jane recalls being "the good adoptee"[4] while growing up. She regularly deferred to others and avoided conflict with her adoptive parents because she feared that if she was not obedient she might be relinquished again. She stayed "little" as opposed to pushing for more individuation from her parents, which would have been based on a stronger sense of self and more confidence in her status as a person becoming an adult. It is interesting to note that in search and reunion, when adoptees seek and possibly face the birth parents they lost, many report that they "finally feel like adults." Achieving adulthood is no easy task for any of us, but for adoptees like Jane there are clearly extra barriers to seeing themselves as adults and being seen as adults in a society that often denies them this important status.

The Ghost Parent Struggle

The thesis of this book is that adoptees have important lifelong connections to their birth parents and that these connections are vital in their development, both emotionally and spiritually. With the exception of Lifton's work, the struggle to explore these "ghost parent" connections has gone unnoticed in much of the literature about adoption. Only recently has it become clear that the love of adoptive parents is *not* enough to bring adopted children along to maturity.[5] There is more to the story of relinquishment and adoption, and that fuller story needs to be acknowledged, understood, and honored for adoptees to grow up well. Nurture, as good as it may be from adoptive parents, is not sufficient for the growth of adopted children. It is the *nature* of their being that must also be appreciated if they are to become healthy, happy adults.

This book presents the argument that the nature of the adoptee includes the reality of relationships with birth parents, which have their own dynamic, their own powerful life in the lives of adoptees. These connections take a variety of forms, all of which are an important part of the development, the more or less *secret* side of development, for adopted persons. They change with time as adoptees mature, and they ebb and flow in intensity, just as relationships with adoptive parents do. But the point here is that these connections are there, there to be understood and interpreted by pastoral caregivers who seek to bring help when problems arise and when normal adoptive development is challenged.

First, the ghost parents of adoptees are lost persons. How infants experience attachment to birth mothers prenatally is a question open to debate, but there is growing evidence[6] that prenatal bonding is real for *both* the birth mother and the infant. If so, then the relinquishment, even at birth, may be a break in bonding with corresponding injury of some form. Postnatal attachment and care enhances the original connection to birth parents and may possibly deepen the pain of loss of those birth parents. However the scenario of initial connection occurs, the struggle of the adoptee begins with a profound moment of loss. In this sense the first loss is the first connection, and it may be a pain too deep to know . . . at least initially.

Second, the ghost parents of adoptees are keepers of identity. In general, much of who we are and how we define ourselves certainly comes from our family experience, our relationships with our parents and our siblings. We internalize the beliefs and values of those around us or we react against them. Either way, we are formed by our interactions with them. Children try to be like the parents they idealize, at least initially. We become our parents to some degree. As we mature we may define ourselves both for and against our parents, but, in either instance, we make use of them in our identity formation. The ghost parents, who are birth parents, also play such a role. They too may be idealized or degraded. They too are part of the adoptees' stories as keepers of parts of their identities. Information about self is not simply information, it is more precious than that. The data about who created us becomes the grist for our development in terms of how we might be proud of ourselves or demean ourselves; either way, it's something important about us. For adoptees the developmental challenge is to learn about and embrace the realities of ghost/birth parents as part of personal history and personal identity. Reality in whatever form must not be avoided, but be faced and understood for growth to continue. The realities of birth parent identities are a form of connection for adoptees regardless of what the content of these identities may be. To the extent that ghost/birth parents are real but unknown and unacknowledged, the task of knowing oneself as an adopted person is difficult.

Third, the ghost parents of adoptees may be roadblocks to attachment and intimacy, at least to the extent that they are unknown and unacknowledged. An adopted child may need to limit or compromise his attachments to others, including adoptive parents and adopted siblings, if his longings for a birth parent in both fantasy and reality occupy his time. Although such longings may be relatively outside of awareness, they may still greatly determine the degree of attachment and the number of connections that an adoptee may allow in his adoptive family. As adolescent development proceeds and the challenge of developing intimate relationships begins, unresolved grieving about these lost parents and an incomplete sense of identity may serve once again to limit real closeness. For one thing, the risk of rejection, relinquishment sensitivity, may loom large for the adoptee. In addition, closeness to others may precipitate awareness of a certain kind of pain about not being close to the birth parents. If closeness hurts, it is natural to avoid it. Such avoidance may serve to maintain connection to ghost parents for adoptees, despite their best intentions to do otherwise.

Fourth, ghost parents are often subjects of fantasy. This has to do with the manner in which adoptees hold their birth parents in their minds. Daydreams, wonderings, musings, and fantasies about birth parents are common experiences for many adoptees.[7] Although such mental creations may not be discussed, they still are an important part of an adoptee's emotional and spiritual experience. These fantasies work to maintain connection to birth parents and to keep hope alive that things can be better. Hoping is a spiritual experience, the belief that there can be a blessing from God in one's future. The form and content of the adoptees' fantasy lives varies widely. Some adoptees report vivid memories of a rescue fantasy in which their birth parents return to take them "home" and, in so doing, solve the problem of grieving. Others report degrading, negative mental images of their birth parents, which suggests a need to hold them at a distance. These examples show that fantasies may be an important, albeit conflictual, form of connection to birth parents for adoptees—another dimension of the secret side of their development.

The ghost parent struggle of adoptees can no longer be denied or go unnoticed. Because more is known about adoptive development specifically, and because shame-based decisions in general always yield new problems down the road of life, it becomes imperative to review our assumptions and understandings about relinquishment and adoption and make some changes. Change is needed, not only in our pastoral approach to adoptees and their families, but also in terms of our challenge to societal attitudes and values about relinquishment and adoption, and to the legal codes that determine rights and privileges for people. The ghost parent struggle has to do not only with the inner workings of the human heart but also with the "principalities and powers" of a world that makes believe that the ghost parent struggle does not exist. It does exist, and adoptees need to be winners in the match between denial and acceptance, between closed records and open access to information, between despair and hope.

A New (Old) Perspective

Adoptees are coming of age. Many no longer accept a less-than-equal status in our society. Current adoption reform is a voice of advocacy for adoptees from two different but complementary perspectives. The first has to do with the mental health and the spiritual well-being of adoptees in terms of maximizing the opportunity for complete development as persons. Secrets about oneself usually hamper growing up well; therefore, the practice of adoption today is becoming less secretive. The mystery of birth history is becoming a story that is told instead of one kept in a dusty suitcase in a closet. The shame that has surrounded pregnancy without marriage is less powerful as a moral force and therefore decisions about relinquishment and adoption are guided by different principles. These principles take the needs of triad members into consideration in healthier ways. Today only 5 percent of single pregnant women relinquish. *The basic paradigm has shifted from that of magically removing shame to minimizing the pain of loss for each triad member.*

Today birth parents bond with their children before surrendering them to other parents (whom they may often choose), making both the connection and the loss more real. Today's more open adoption practice means that many birth parents have contact with the adoptive family and know whether their birth children are healthy. They are partners in the formation of adoptive families. Adoptive parents sometimes feel threatened by this, but they are learning to see these relationships differently and respectfully instead of avoiding them. And, most importantly for our concerns, infants and children who are relinquished and adopted today lose less. In the more open adoption experience they have more information about their birth parents and, therefore, spend less time in fantasy about them. With less secrecy there is less shame, and this means less internalization of that shame. Self-esteem has a better chance for survival.

The second voice that is being heard as adoptees come of age today is a human rights call for justice on the adoptee's behalf. Prior to this century, adoption records were public records. Minnesota was the first to close them in 1917. State after state followed the lead. In Colorado, adoption records were closed in 1949. These were retroactive decisions, meaning that *all* adoption records became closed records. Adoptees were shut off from their roots, their ancestry, their bloodlines, their medical stories—all parts of themselves. Now advocates of adoption reform are petitioning the courts all across the country to open these records in a manner that is respectful of birth parent privacy, while allowing for possible reunion if both parties consent. Many adoptees believe that they have a right to know their birth stories whether they exercise that right or not. They are coming of age as adults who are insisting that they have the same rights to their stories as their nonadopted peers. They are not whining like children; they are speaking as adults who know that they have rights to their individual heritages.

Adoptees are coming of age too in terms of the questions that are being asked about them in the literature. As far back as 1943, social worker and adoption specialist Florence Clothier discussed the problem that she saw adopted children facing:

> The child who does not grow up with his own biological parents, who does not even know them or anyone of his own blood, is an individual who has lost the thread of family continuity. A deep identification with our forebears, as experienced originally in the mother-child relationship, gives us our most fundamental security. The child's repeated discoveries that the mother from whom he has been biologically separated will continue to warm him, nourish him, and protect him pours into the very structure of his personality a stability and a reassurance that he is safe, even in this new, alien world.
>
> Every adopted child, at some point in his development, has been deprived of this primitive relationship with his mother. This trauma and the severing of the individual from his racial antecedents lie at the core of what is peculiar to the psychology of the adopted child. The adopted child presents all the complications in social and emotional development seen in the own child. But the ego of the adopted child, in addition to all the normal demands made upon it, is called upon to compensate for the wound left by the loss of the biological mother. Later on this appears as an unknown void, separating the adopted child from his fellows whose blood ties bind them to the past as well as to the future.[8]

Clothier had identified the dilemma of the relinquished child, well over fifty years ago, and she answered a primary question in the literature at that time: Does adoption put children at greater risk for psychological difficulties? As the answer to this question appeared to be yes in study after study, the next question emerged: Well, then, when should children be told of their adoption? Arguments were drawn on both sides in terms of telling early or waiting until latency (ages seven through ten) to tell in order that the child be psychologically and cognitively able to handle what may be difficult information. Without a definitive answer to this question, a substantial body of literature developed around the question of identity: Do adoptees have special struggles with their identity, particularly in adolescence? Next, the literature began to review the depths of lifelong grieving involved in adoption for all of the parties of the triad. The question, How much mourning is involved in adoption?, has recently given way to new interest in grief resolution, specifically in terms of search and reunion. Coming then full circle, from secrecy to openness and to the full disclosure of reunion, the more recent literature examines the questions about the benefits and difficulties of finding birth parents. And, finally, with the preponderant argument that search and reunion can be a useful choice, the adoption literature has moved to the question of advocacy, declaring the rights of adoptees to know their own birth histories, medical records, and the identity of birth parents.[9]

Today's question in the field of adoption concerns openness for all triad members. How can relinquishment and adoption be organized in such a way as to minimize the pain of loss and to maximize positive relationships among the triad members as *resources* for the mental health and spiritual well-being of the adoptee? The adoptee is coming of age as the person of major concern in adoption practice. In a real and substantial way, openness in adoption practice is now happening and benefiting adoptees. There's less lost and more known and accepted in today's adoption story.

Returning once more to Carl's story, he came back two years later for more pastoral counseling. He had held a knife to his throat, announcing to his adoptive mother that he was not sure he wanted to live anymore. Life hurt too much, even at age thirteen. He was struggling with friends and struggling with schoolwork. It sounded like his heart was simply not in his life. And once again he reported that he missed Patty. His birth-mother longings were once again before him in a powerful way. He wrote her this letter:

Dear Patty,

I am writing because I am struggling in school. My grades haven't been very good. I have been thinking about you lately. Since I've been thinking about you I have had some problems with my parents. That's why I have not been doing well in school. I have had this wish that you could be my parent. I've also thought that you could save me from school in my wishes. I have this wish that you could save me from my other parents. The rest of my life is OK in reality. Some day I wish that I will see you in person to speak with you. I hope you are doing well. I have a couple of questions to ask you. I was wondering would you make me do homework? Would I have to be in bed at a special time? Would you have rules for me in life?

Love, Carl

His letter is a plea for help in terms of resolving the grieving that was so much a part of Carl's life. He speaks openly of his rescue fantasy and is working to accept the reality that it will not occur. And as he closes, he asks her for help in terms of shutting the door between them. Hearing her say that she *would* have rules for him would help him resolve the fantasy that she would not. Carl was struggling to make it work, but he needed Patty to nudge him away, toward his adoptive family, toward his real day-to-day life.

This story illustrates how caring birth parents and open adoptive parents can be useful resources for adoptees like Carl. Adoptees are coming of age as people with legitimate needs for human connection with the people who gave them life.

Reversing the Orphan Trains

Between the years 1853 and 1929 the Children's Aid Society of New York City placed more than one hundred thousand children on trains, sending them to forty-seven of the fifty states.[10] It began as the work of a pastor from Connecticut, the Rev. Charles Loring Brace, who came to New York for his training in ministry and took interest in the plight of the many orphans of the city. He found these children sleeping on street corners, in boatyard docks, and in old buildings, children with no resource but begging. Brace believed that the "kind Christian homes" of rural America would have great interest in providing shelter for these children, giving them a chance in life. These children had economic value that could be exchanged for homes in which to live. Young boys and girls were placed on trains on Tuesdays with arrivals set for Saturdays to prepare for viewing on Sundays in local churches. They were literally "put up" for adoption on old crates at train stations. Children were stripped of anything that could possibly identify them and promised a new life in the country. Addresses of parents and relatives were taken away. Because they were considered the progeny of "bad blood" (it was believed that the blood "carried" the bad behavior), the less known about their histories the better. Local committees set up screening for prospective adoptive families, but always there were more children than families available. Many children ran away.

On May 31, 1929, the last orphan train left New York for Clarksville, Texas. Times had changed, and it was no longer considered a good thing to do. Ideas about the virtue of work for children had given way to the benefits of play in their development. Concern shifted from their economic value in the factory or on the farm to the importance of their emotional well-being. Brace, in his compassion for these children of the streets, had tried to find a better way for them to live. The values and assumptions about persons that guided his decision, and the thinking of many Children's Aid societies at the turn of the century, certainly had benevolent intent, but nevertheless the orphan trains left little hearts hurt and empty. Brace made this ambivalent comment in the face of so many children growing up in rags: "The human soul is difficult to interfere with. You hesitate how far you should go."[11]

Relinquishment and adoption have, first of all, to do with the hearts of children. Equipping infants and young girls and young boys to grow up well means giving them not only the care and nurture that all children need, but also, if they are adoptees, giving them their stories. Of necessity, relinquishment and adoption have to do with "interference" with the human soul. Bringing that interference to an absolute minimum is appropriate pastoral care for the hearts of children often too young to know their left hand from their right hand, to know their birth story from their adoption story, to know their several parents from their God.

Chapter Two

The Necessary Mourning
of Relinquishment

*Adoptive families are formed out of loss. It always hurts to lose
someone. I think that all my life I knew that I was sad. I just didn't
know why.*

—*Sarah, twenty-two-year-old adoptee*

A Healing Moment

It was a humid summer night in northwest Iowa. For Travis it was going to be a fun night, so he thought. He and his third-grade friends were
all gathered in the front row of the small-town auditorium with popcorn
in hand, ready for the concert to begin. "Glad," a men's chorus, was about
to begin the evening's entertainment. Nearly the whole town had shown
up for the show. Sitting in the front row was the usual routine for the third-
grade gang. Moms and dads were back a few rows with watchful eyes.
Pleasant melodies cut away the boredom of the summer night. But then
the group paused and spoke about children in third-world countries who
had no parents because of drought and disease. They made a specific reference to Uganda, where as many as 80 percent of village children might
soon be parentless because of the AIDS virus. They then dedicated a song
to these boys and girls across the world and began to sing. Travis slouched
into the back of his seat, put his bag of popcorn on the floor, and his eyes
began to well up with tears from deep within. At age eight he knew why.
When it hurt too much for him to tolerate being alone, Travis rose from
his seat and began to walk right in front of the stage to the aisle and headed
up, before the eyes of everyone, to the row where his parents sat. They
wondered as he walked their way what might be the reason. This was not
like him. He loved to be with his friends, and the front row was base camp

for their fun together. As he got closer, even in the dim light, his mother and father could both see the tears flowing down his cheeks. Travis crawled into his mother's lap and in the broken voice of a hurting child said, "Mom, I miss my birth mom." With tears now in her own eyes she responded, "Honey, I know that you do." Dad squeezed Travis's hand in silent support.

There is grief in the heart of every adoptee. In Travis's case, at that moment, the mourning that *necessarily* comes with relinquishment was right in the center of his eight-year-old awareness. Talk about children without parents in Africa triggered his own heartfelt reality that he too was a child without parents, without the ghost parents of his beginnings, despite the care and connection of his adoptive folks. This is the first and greatest pain of relinquishment, the truth that there are other parents out there somewhere whom the adoptee may hold in his heart but has lost in his day-to-day life. *The grieving of this loss is critical for healthy adoptive development*, as is any grieving that must be done in the face of personal tragedy. And it is here, especially, where the adoptee is at great risk depending on whether adoptive parents communicate the freedom and permission to cry in their arms about lost birth parents. In Travis's story it is clear that he knew he *could* get up and find his parents and that they would accept his sadness. Travis knew that he *could* grieve and release some of his inner suffering in the arms of his adoptive parents, who would support him by being sad and by weeping with him. In so doing he was indeed on the road to being OK.

But what if all of this had gone differently? What if Travis's adoptive mother had not accepted her own personal pain that comes with infertility? For her and her husband, there were several years of sorrow about being a nonconceptive couple, unable to complete the dreams that came with their marriage. *Children by birth cannot be replaced by children by adoption.* The wished-for birth child was never to be born to them. This is loss, deeply heartfelt loss. And some such couples adopt, not simply as an alternative way to build a family, but as a way to replace, without grieving for, the lost longed-for child by birth. Had this been the case with Travis's parents, they might have given him the message, subtle or not so subtle, that he should *not* miss his birth mother or his birth father just as they should not miss their never-to-be-born birth son or daughter. And, in this collusion of making believe that things are different from reality, both adoptive parents and adoptees may be caught in the emotional and spiritual trap of never-released grief, the number-one threat to adoptees and their families.

Again, what if for some reason Travis had learned that it was not OK for him to be sad about his birth parent losses? What if it were not safe for him to cry or mention his feelings and fantasies about these ghost parents? Given the basic premise of this book, which is that relinquishment is a real grief that must be acknowledged and managed, where would the grieving go? The answer for most adoptees is that it would go outside of awareness. Without the support of adoptive parents the adoptee is left unable to grieve this loss. Good parents are resources to our children. Whatever the children's pain might be, we need to be present with them in such a fashion that they learn that their emotions are acceptable, not to be feared but to be respected and experienced so that they become important parts of a person's story. If Travis had learned not to talk about relinquishment or birth parents or adoption because these topics were unacceptable, he would have been in the (neurotic) bind of becoming anxious about his experience. He might have had impulses to be sad and then blocked those impulses, pushing the sadness away because of a belief that it was unacceptable or even wrong to feel such a thing. To honor the emotion might have meant dishonor or disloyalty to his parents (adoptees often report feeling this conflict). Then, denying the sadness, which is the *normal* mourning that accompanies loss, becomes the safest option, at least for a child struggling to make sense out of the confusion that comes with having two sets of parents, "one on the inside and one on the outside."

Travis was fortunate. He did not have to deny his sadness. His parents did not make relinquishment an anxiety-producing issue. Instead, that warm night in Iowa became a warm moment of healing for Travis. In the process of grieving we bring to mind precisely the person that we miss dearly. We create and recreate this image of a person *as many times as we need to* in order to experience the feelings of loss that accompany that image. Perhaps a thousand times we remember, we reconstruct the image or the memory of someone important. For Travis this was one of those important times of mourning, of feeling his birth parent sadness, which is part of the story of healthy adoptive development. He cried the tears that adoptees need to cry at some time and some level in order to make sense of their unusual realities. And for Travis, because his parents understood the significance of the moment, the moment went well.

Relinquishment — the Primal Wound?

Just exactly how is it that relinquishment hurts an infant or a small child or a not-so-small child like Travis? How is relinquishment an experience that *does* matter in what may be a negative, painful way? Once again it is important to think about relinquishment, not simply as an event in the hospital or courtroom, but as an ongoing experience in the heart of a child. Relinquishment in this sense is a breaking of an attachment to a mother that has its own life in terms of time and its own lingering effects on a child's development. And relinquishment may begin even in the womb.

After twenty-nine years of wondering about her baby, Carolyn answered the phone one day and heard her birth daughter, Sandy, on the line. This moment, in the process of search and reunion with a birth parent, is almost always a profound and deeply emotional moment. For Carolyn it meant the end to her ongoing concern that her birth daughter's life would be all right. It meant the beginning of a new relationship in reality that would heal some of the hurt that birth mothers sometimes carry for a lifetime about their decisions to relinquish and make a plan for adoption. In the course of the conversations, which were intense in the days and weeks following their initial contact, the two of them talked often about what they each were like, and shared their likes and dislikes. At one point while talking Sandy mentioned to her birth mother that her favorite music was what she called "Handel's water music." Carolyn could hardly believe Sandy's words. They triggered for her an emotional return to her days at the Booth Memorial Home[1] where she was sent after becoming pregnant. She told Sandy about the long days when she would sit in a rocking chair listening to Handel's *Water Music*, wondering what would happen to her baby.

Prenatal Pain?

Carolyn and Sandy may have *both* heard the same music in the limited time of their life together before Sandy's birth. Prenatal life is that of a fetus becoming a person. Human experience does not begin at the moment of delivery and birth, but well before a child is born. Prenatal life is life, and especially in the sixth through the ninth months of development, a fetus in utero begins the process of becoming a person. We know, for example, that after twenty-four weeks of growth a fetus is able to hear. For our purpose, the question of fetal consciousness is important, not only in terms of the pleasant idea of mother and baby hearing the same music during pregnancy but also in terms of the more difficult question of determining how the fetus-becoming-person experiences relationship with the birth mother. The birth mother may be in distress because of her unplanned pregnancy and because of the ambivalence and anguish of dealing with the possibility of relinquishment. Certainly, then, the pain of relinquishment for the baby may begin in the womb.

The presence of pain, of course, depends on whether there is some form of experiencing self in the developing fetus. As the fetus develops prenatally, how much can be known as experience? Memory traces such as those that Sandy "recalls" around Handel's *Water Music* are not uncommon from the sixth through the ninth month of gestation. But the critical question here has to do with how the fetus experiences things. If the experiencing self emerges only later on in development, even sometime after birth, then what happens prenatally matters less in terms of the loss of connection to a birth mother. However, if there *is* an experiencing self, even early in fetal development, then what happens prenatally matters a lot. It is possible, then, that the fetus could be aware that something is amiss in its mother's heart. And, if this is the case, then prenatally there could be a loss of the vital connection to the birth mother. Relinquishment may mean prenatal pain.

Dr. Thomas Verny, in *The Secret Life of the Unborn Child*, argues that indeed this may be the case. He believes that a great deal is going on in terms of prenatal development that, up until recently, has not been seriously considered. In contrast to Freud's notion that self-awareness comes in either the second or third year of life around the time of Oedipal conflict,[2] Verny suggests that the self of a child is very much there prenatally.[3] He bases his argument on a host of international studies on prenatal life from which he draws several foundational conclusions. The first and most obvious conclusion is that birth is not the beginning of emotional life for infants just as it is not the beginning of physical life for them. To think that it is, is to ignore much of prenatal reality. Especially in the last months of gestation, they are persons in relationship. The second and perhaps equally important conclusion Verny draws is that the emotional well-being of the mother is critical to the physical and emotional well-being of the baby *before* it is born.

Verny reports correlations between the basic love that a mother has for her child and the physical well-being of that child both before, during, and after its birth. He cites studies that suggest that mothers who report negative attitudes toward their babies have more medical difficulties during pregnancy and higher rates of premature, low-weight, or emotionally disturbed infants. Verny suggests that one explanation for these correlations may be found in the data connecting emotional stress in the mother's experience and unusually high levels of neurohormonal secretions, which change the environment of the fetus in a negative way.[4] These secretions, most often triggered by stress, may heighten an infant's susceptibility to emotional distress, and they create a prenatal environment in which there may be a greater incidence of physical problems such as gastrointestinal difficulties. He also discusses the manner in which the hypothalamus gland functions as the "body's emotional regulator"[5] and how the emotional state of the mother affects this gland directly in terms of the mechanisms that control the endocrine and autonomic nervous systems. Verny cites several studies that show clear correlations between emotional instability on the part of the mother and hypothalamic vulnerability, which may have a direct effect both physically and emotionally on the prenatal infant.[6] A good deal of evidence suggests that the physical and emotional well-being of the prenatal infant depends on the emotional health of its mother.

How might relinquishment, then, be experienced prenatally by the fetus? Most birth mothers who choose to relinquish their children do so with greatly mixed emotions. They report feeling guilt, anger, and sadness. To the extent that they are *healthy*, they hurt in regard to the decision to surrender a baby for adoption. It is a very painful experience. Our question here has to do with how a prenatal infant, especially in the last months of pregnancy, might *experience* the mother's emotional suffering. If Verny's observations have validity, then it is reasonable to believe that maternal anxiety surrounding the decision to relinquish could directly affect the prenatal life of the child. *Relinquishment would hurt even before the adoptee is born.*

Not only would there be unfortunate chemical or physical changes in the environment, but, just as importantly, there may be a compromised attachment to the mother if she withdraws emotionally from her child as she anticipates relinquishment, despite her own best conscious efforts to be and stay connected. Anticipatory grief may get in the way. For instance, she may talk to her baby less, rub her stomach less, communicate in a variety of ways that she herself is in distress. Verny describes, in a chapter entitled "Interuterine Bonding," the prenatal self as very much an emerging emotional self, responding with increasing interest to the relationship with the mother, enjoying, for example, the sound of her heartbeat. He describes the ways in which important communication occurs between fetus-becoming-person and the mother. For example, a baby may kick in response to discomfort or loud noise or some other disturbance. Or a baby may be soothed by the sound of music. Verny describes what he calls "sympathetic communication"[7] as the sense that an attentive mother may have for the emotional state of her baby. Her voice may calm the baby *before* it is born just as it may do so after a baby is born. But, once again, if she is dealing with the anxieties involved in relinquishment, she may be less attentive to such nuances of development as she anticipates the loss of the very child she is bringing to life. And somehow the prenatal infant may know, and in so doing, may have to deal with the first impingements of relinquishment on his not-yet-born experience.

Baby Grief?

Social worker Nancy Verrier has coined the term "primal wound" to describe what she believes to be the narcissistic injury that occurs when a baby is taken from its mother and placed in the arms of adoptive parents, who are initially strangers, no matter how caring they may be.

> When this natural evolution [of birth mother and fetus bonding] is interrupted by a postnatal separation, the resultant experience of abandonment and loss is indelibly imprinted upon the unconscious minds of these children, causing that which I call the 'primal wound.'[8]

Drawing on her research as a clinician as well as her role as both an adoptive mother and biological mother, Verrier asserts that this primal wound "affects the adoptee's sense of Self and often manifests in a sense of loss, basic mistrust, anxiety and depression, emotional and behavioral problems, and difficulties in relationships with significant others."[9] In contrast to the clinical judgments of adoption practitioners over the past several decades, she asserts that the adopted child is indeed a wounded child who is in need of help in terms of managing the pain that comes with this abandonment. In *The Primal Wound* she focuses on the depth of this loss and its profound impact on adoptees' development as children, as adolescents, and as adults who must manage the pain of this wound. Verrier, like Verny, sees the infant, soon to be legally relinquished, as a person with forty weeks of profound connection to its birth mother. She argues that breaking this vital attachment is a trauma, the proportions of which are simply unknown and unknowable. But the trauma is real. The normal and understandable results of this trauma, she says, are: basic anxieties, fears of further loss and abandonment (relinquishment sensitivity), psychosomatic difficulties, and struggles with trust in relationships. She cautions that treating these "symptoms" as pathological means misunderstanding them and therefore failing to be helpful in the emotional development of the adopted person.[10]

The point is that the cry of the relinquished infant is a real human cry of real human suffering. Janice, an adoptive mother, sat in my office in tears describing her silent disappointment in her experience with her daughter, who seemed to fight her every attempt at the initial bonding and ongoing attachment for which she as a mother longed. The early excitement of bringing Cari home changed quickly into extended sleepless nights of wondering what was wrong with her as a mother. The struggle with infertility had been painful in its own right: her body would not cooperate in maintaining a pregnancy. After three miscarriages it hurt too much to try again. And now adoption was bringing her back to those same feelings of inadequacy. This time she wondered why her love was not enough to make the needed connection with Cari. She recalled the awkward moment of meeting. Her first impressions were mixed because two-week-old Cari not only cried but screamed in her arms at the agency where their relationship was "born." This was supposed to be the moment of love at first sight, the birth of lifelong heartfelt connection that would give Cari a home and Janice a child. It was supposed to be wonderful but, in truth, it was painful. Both Janice and her husband knew at some important level that Cari did not want this. Her cries were a protest against her adoption, letting them know that this was *not* what she as adoptee wanted for the moment or for her life.

In Verrier's terms, Cari was dealing with her primal wound in the only way that she as an infant could, by *not* allowing anyone else to replace the birth mother who gave her life, who talked to her at night, who sang to her in the daytime, who moved sideways when Cari was in prenatal discomfort, and who wept deeply three days after her birth, after nursing her, as she signed papers of relinquishment and hugged her goodbye. No, Cari was not up for this new arrangement, although her adoptive parents certainly were. Instead, she fought it fiercely, screaming no to the great exchange. Janice was not inadequate, she simply did not understand that Cari was not yet able or willing to give her a chance. Cari needed to protest the primal wound of relinquishment before she would consider finding a way to heal.

When in our theorizing about prenatal and postnatal experience, we *think* about babies as persons who have the increasing capacity to be experiencing selves, we must face the painful possibility of significant injury to the hearts and souls of these very young persons. And if we *see* them in this light, we may begin to understand how exceedingly difficult both relinquishment and adoption may be for them. As birth parents, we are asking a great deal of them in terms of managing and accepting our decision to release them to the parenting of others. As adoptive parents, we are asking a great deal of them in terms of grieving their loss and allowing us to care for them, to let us into their lives as new resources for their care. And as members of society who have a social concern for their welfare, we are asking a great deal of them in terms of allowing adoption to be the solution to their need for care. In all instances their protest *against* adoption is at least understandable. In so many ways it hurts to be relinquished. Baby grief is real grief, and we can be much more helpful to them if we have ears to hear their suffering.

Awareness—the Second Wound?

Imagine, if you will, what it is like for adoptees to finally figure out that they are indeed *adopted* people. Imagine what happens in the course of growing up when a relinquished and adopted child is able for the first time to "get it" that there are real but "ghost" parents out there somewhere in this world who gave up their role as parents, who signed him or her away to someone else. Imagine what happens when this wave of awareness washes over the heart and soul of the young adoptee?

Sally, at age seven, was such a person. Her third-grade world was in many ways a good world. Her adoptive parents were open to her struggles and talked often about relinquishment and adoption with her. As far back as she could remember, she had known she was adopted, and her first report to me was that that was OK with her. Along with her adopted brother Todd, two years younger, she was part of a reasonably healthy adoptive family. Her adoptive parents seemed to be doing all the right things. Nevertheless, in the middle of her third-grade year, Sally began to slip academically. Her teacher reported that she was less attentive in the classroom.

Sally seemed easily distracted and less interested in what was happening in class. Several angry outbursts on the playground led to new difficulties in her third-grade friendships. She was beginning to isolate herself from others. Her teacher felt that she was somehow losing Sally, and at that point she called her parents for a conference, wondering if things were OK at home. Puzzled and concerned, her parents consulted me regarding Sally. After all, up to this point Sally had been a great student and in their minds a "great kid." They reported to the teacher that at home Sally seemed fine although quieter, which they had attributed to growing up. They did not know what to make of this turn of events in Sally's life. The teacher told them of one scenario when Sally's friends were all playing jump rope on the playground and twice invited Sally to join them. She declined and told them she "just wanted to be alone for a while."

Sally was depressed, *normally* depressed because she was grieving. It is not uncommon for adoptees to experience a wave of melancholy in the third or fourth grade no matter how supportive and attentive their parents may be. There is a clearly defined reason for this. When children are about seven or eight years old, their ability to conceptualize comes into play. Prior to this age a child is usually described as a "concrete thinker" who is able to understand things in literal terms. To grasp ideas, the abstract, is a new awareness. Subjects like the permanence of death do not make sense to a child up to this point in life, but with the dawn of this new level of awareness concepts like relinquishment and adoption begin to make sense. And with a new capacity to conceptualize comes the second wound of relinquishment, namely, awareness that there are in reality another set of parents, real birth parents, who are indeed missing in the adoptee's life. And *this new awareness hurts*. Sally, with this new awareness of loss, was grieving for her birth parents, especially her birth mother, whom she mentioned once conversation about these things began. She would look out the window of her bedroom, wondering where her birth mother was, wondering what she looked like, and, most importantly to Sally, wondering why her birth mother had "given her away." No explanation could take her pain away, but she, in her seven-year-old mind, wanted to know. For Sally, as for many young adoptees, it hurt when finally she figured it out. Experiencing relinquishment both prenatally and postnatally in a very primitive, preverbal way is something that a baby's primal heart and body knows. In early latency, another way of knowing occurs when a child's mind makes sense of the loss of birth parents. And then relinquishment hurts again.

David M. Brodzinsky, a researcher at Rutgers University, has studied the adopted child's understandings of adoption at various young ages.[11] He and his colleagues report on an extensive study of two hundred children, half of whom were adoptees. The subjects ranged in age from four to thirteen. The findings are of significant interest in terms of understanding the cognitive and emotional experience of the adoptee. First of all, although one would guess that adoptees heard much more about adoption than their non-adopted peers, adoptees at these ages did *not* know more about what adoption was. Few six-year-olds were able to differentiate between birth and adoption as ways to enter a family. Instead they tended to fuse the two concepts together. For example,

> Adoption means you go to try to get a baby and if you can't you can't. [Where do you get the baby that you adopt?] From your vagina or your tummy. [Whose vagina or tummy?] The baby's mommy. [Is the baby adopted?] Yes . . . cause the mommy has it now. It came out of her. [Are all babies adopted?] Yep.[12]

As children grow older, according to this study, they begin to make sense of the concept of adoption, and as they do, they initially trust the parents' promises about permanence (around age seven) to the degree that they can understand it. But as maturing continues and the realization occurs that there are real other parents (around age eight), the permanence of adoption comes under question and adoptees wonder whether they might be taken back. "Biological parents are seen as having the potential for reclaiming guardianship over the child at some future but unspecified time."[13] Brodzinsky found that children at age eight or nine characterize adoption as a legal arrangement that includes some sense of permanence. By age eleven or twelve boys and girls were clear about the legality and the permanence of adoption. All of this is to say that, depending on the age at which relinquishment and adoption are discussed, a child will have a different understanding of what these words mean. And appreciating the *children's* point of view is obviously critical in terms of understanding what might make them sad.

Telling about Adoption

A well-intentioned mother sat down with her adopted three-year-old daughter, Suzanne, to tell her the story of her relinquishment and adoption. Beginning this conversation was somewhat awkward for the mother because of her fears about hurting Suzanne's feelings. She told the story of Molly, another woman who lived far away in another state. Molly was Suzannne's birth mother, which meant that Suzanne first grew as a baby in Molly's tummy. She went on to describe how after Suzanne was born she came to live with her and Suzanne's daddy, Bill. Puzzled by all this, Suzanne seemed more interested in playing with her dolls. Suzanne then quipped to her adoptive mother, "Mom, Molly is the name of Gramma's horse." Based upon Brodzinsky's insights into the cognitive abilities of children, it is clear

that this well-intentioned adoptive mother was speaking in words yet unknown to her three-year-old daughter. Suzanne could not *get* what her
mother was talking about. And indeed it would be years before this child
would comprehend the meanings of relinquishment and adoption. More
than anything else she probably sensed her mother's anxiety and cut the
conversation short.

The issue of telling is important. Telling children about their relinquishment and adoption raises questions about honesty in relationships and
risks potential injury to the hearts and souls of little children. It is a challenge that makes adoptive parents anxious, perhaps because of uncertainty
about an adoptee's reaction to this "news." In early adoption literature, several psychoanalytic theorists held sway, advising adoptive parents *not* to tell
their children too early. They believed that such information at age two or
three or four would constitute a significant narcissistic injury, the proportions of which would be too great for a young child to manage. Learning of
relinquishment and adoption too early would indeed interfere with "normal" development in several ways, they thought. In 1960, psychiatrist
Marshall D. Schechter wrote that he observed problems in his adopted
patients in terms of symptom formations, the splitting of parental objects,
and "grave difficulties" with superego and ego-ideal formation when told
too early of their relinquishment and adoption.[14] The trauma caused by
this revelation was too severe for a child to handle prior to latency age,
Schechter wrote. Similarly, psychiatrist Herbert Weider argued that dis-
closing this information to an adoptee too early in life was damaging in several ways. "Immaturity and inability to clearly comprehend or master the
implications produced confusion, anxiety, shame, and rage, with lasting effects on the adoptee's personality and intellect."[15] This prevailing attitude
made telling all the more anxiety-producing for adoptive parents.

More recent wisdom on the subject suggests the opposite, that adoptive
parents tell their children about their adoption early and often, over and
over, being aware that the child will probably be unable to understand until a later stage of cognitive development. In this sense Brodzinsky's insights
into a child's comprehension of the meanings of relinquishment and adoption have been important. The telling that is advised today is more of a
process of adoptive family life (as the family tells its story). One advantage
to this kind of telling is that it gives the *parents* the opportunity to become
comfortable with the idea. It may be that the greatest challenge here, given
what we know about children's limited abilities to understand, is for adoptive parents themselves to practice talking about these things so that they
become increasingly comfortable with their own feelings about the circumstances surrounding their decisions to adopt. For, as the parents become more at ease, more accepting of their own stories, their children, the
adoptees, will sense the freedom to ask the questions and get the answers

that will help them understand. Children of adoption who sense such permission to ask are enabled to grieve birth parent losses honestly and accurately. As they come to understand the reality of their stories, they also know that they can indeed crawl up into a mother's lap and announce, "Mommy, I miss my birth mom," holding a father's hand.

Lost Pieces in Adolescence—the Third Wounding?

With roughly one-half of marriages failing in America today, many teens are growing up in single-parent homes and are challenged to deal with the grief that surrounds divorce. Ellen was one of those children. At age fifteen she was openly angry about the breakup of her parents' marriage of nearly twenty years. In typical adolescent fashion Ellen let the world know of her great protest. She first headed off to the shopping mall with her father's (secretly taken) credit card and, in one afternoon, charged nearly seven hundred dollars for new shirts and sweaters and fancy underwear. What a way to let them know. Talking about her anger seemed to do little to alleviate it. She was not about to accept this state of affairs (yes, her father had one). She openly blamed both parents for splitting up, and in different ways she punished them. To her mother she spoke little, even though only the two of them lived in the "new" apartment. The sword of silence effectively brought her mom to her emotional knees. Self-protectively her mother withdrew and both of them lost an important connection. Ellen's rampage of emotional warfare went on into shoplifting, ditching school, pot smoking, and sexual intercourse with two boys whom she hardly knew. Finally, referred by friends who were worried about her, she came to see me to talk about her angry life.

The sting of divorce had cut deeply into Ellen's heart because, among other things, she was a relinquished and adopted person. Not only was she faced with dealing with the abandonment that divorce feels like to a child, despite the best intentions of the separated parents, but also she had to deal with the echo of birth parent losses. The impending divorce felt like a second round of losing parents, a second time of feeling like an orphan, and so Ellen's rage went deep. Now at age fifteen she had to somehow return to the moment when she was two weeks old and lost her first set of parents. She had difficult, double-duty therapy to do in terms of managing the losses in her life.

If sadness seems to be the heartfelt response of adopted children, as when Travis crawled up into his mother's lap, anger may be the characteristic response of adopted adolescents. At this time in an adoptee's life a renewed awareness of loss may "go off like a bomb" amidst the storms of adolescence. Identity formation (à la Erik Erikson—an adoptee who learned of his adoption at age sixteen and renamed himself)[16] is one of the central developmental tasks of teenage life. This will be discussed in detail in the next chapter. For now, let us simply note that an adoptee who asks questions about identity will *not* get answers if birth history and ethnic identity and all the rest of his or her roots are locked in a closed adoption file. Then, not only is the adopted teen at a disadvantage in terms of missing pieces of the puzzle of personal identity, but that teen is also grieving, perhaps angrily, because something and someone important was lost. That hurts.

One teenage adoptee, in reference to his irritation with not knowing anybody who looked like he did, put it this way, "I was adopted, not born." For him there was indeed an important part of himself that he did not know, and this loss was painful. In adolescence we define ourselves, but we usually do so by way of reference points to parents. We adopt and adapt certain traits of our mothers and fathers which we like, and we internalize them, and we reject and object to other traits that we dislike. We both identify with and differentiate from the parents or caregivers who brought us up. But what if half of our stories are missing? What if the mental representations of the parents who created us are "lost"? What if the building blocks that are absolutely necessary for putting together a solid sense of self are just plain missing for the adopted adolescent who wants to create a self with self-esteem? The losses that accompany relinquishment and adoption become, once again, profoundly real and really painful. Another wave of grieving may wash over the heart of the struggling adolescent and show itself in angry, open defiance—such as running off with Dad's credit card to the mall. It hurts to lose parents and it hurts to not know who you are. Once again, relinquishment takes its toll.

Echoes in Adulthood—Fourth-Level Hurts?

Finding one's place in the world is an adult endeavor. Psychiatrist Steven Nickman, in an article entitled "Losses in Adoption,"[17] comments:

> The circumstances of being adopted are a special case of universal dilemmas. . . . We all wonder where we came from and how we will meet our end; these are the primary questions from which all religion and philosophy spring. How do we contemplate a past in which we played no part and a future which will proceed without us? Blood ties attenuate the pain of these questions for most people; adoptees, however, are brought closer to a sense of basic anxiety about their place in the world.[18]

Finding one's place in the world is usually more difficult for adoptees. Even if adoptees have weathered all the storms of development described so far, and even if they have done well in terms of the necessary mourning that comes with relinquishment, they nevertheless have more with which to deal in adult life. Adopted adults, who have grown up differently in terms of the twoness of being relinquished and adopted, walk along in life with the scars of the losses involved and wonder whether the pain of their stories may return.

When Barb visited her doctor because of some dizzy spells she was having, she remembered the many times when, in filling out medical history questionnaires, she had answered, "Don't know—adopted." But this time it took on new importance when she learned of the possibility of multiple sclerosis. The origins of this disease are unknown. But for Barb the not knowing felt different, more ominous, more critical. What was her birth mother's medical story? What about the possibility of cancer? What other inherited conditions or genetic diseases possibly threatened her future? These unknowns were now increasingly unacceptable. And at this point Barb decided to search for her birth mother in order to fill in the blanks on the medical page. Her hurt has turned to irritation, and once again relinquishment and adoption have their sting in adult life.

Even the project of securing nonidentifying information proved difficult. There was a fifty-dollar fee for the paperwork for information that she felt *belonged* to her. She waited six weeks for the two-page document to come. It told her of her German-Irish descent on her birth mother's side and French-Italian on her birth father's. Both were high school students at the time of her birth. But no medical information was given about either. The file to basic medical and most personal history was locked. For an additional four hundred dollars Barb petitioned the Denver Juvenile Court to assign her case to a state-appointed Confidential Intermediary who could open the adoption records and pursue reunion on Barb's behalf. However, the local judge, Dana Wakefield, had ordered a stay on such requests because he believed that they were unconstitutional in terms of violating the (promised) anonymity of the birth parents involved.

Several years later, when the stay was overruled by the state supreme court, more than 350 such cases were presented to intermediaries for review. But Barb once again knew how it felt to be relinquished and adopted. She felt diminished in a world where others took basic birth knowledge for granted. Now there was more grief to be grieved because of her mixed status in society and her sense of suffering the consequences of a decision in which she never had a voice. The lingering injuries of injustice were once again on her mind in adulthood.

Adult adoptees often report that they are sensitive to rejection in adult life because of the earlier pain of relinquishment. "Relinquishment sensitivity," described in chapter 1, is sometimes simply part of life for an adoptee. Feeling vulnerable and hesitant in relationships may cause adoptees to reject the partner during courtship. Fear of rejection (relinquishment sensitivity) may stop the adoptee from taking risks in employment, both in seeking jobs and in keeping jobs. Overhearing comments in public about problems of children of adoption may hurt in ways that go unnoticed in the crowd. But the sting is there for the adopted adult, a hurt that is seldom understood in our culture. Such are the pains from sensitivity and from insensitivity that are often part of adoptive adult life.

To Grieve or Not to Grieve?

Nothing hurts like relinquishment hurts. To know in the very core of your being that from the first moments of your being you were rejected is a wound that may never completely heal. The question of this chapter and ultimately of this book is whether we in the nonadopted population can care for relinquished and adopted persons in a manner that helps them grieve. They will only know that they are entirely loved if we as pastors and counselors as well as family and friends can embrace them at the center of their own hearts and feel with them, at least to some degree, how much it hurts to *not* be sure whether they were ever loved in the first place. Even if they were loved, in their experience they were not loved enough to be claimed for life by their birth parents. Our ability to be empathic to this kind of original rejection determines whether adoptees can receive the support they need to do the grieving they must do.

Not grieving has been the norm. During the past fifty years our society has not been able to see the catch-22 in which relinquishment and adoption place a child. And, without permission to be sad, adoptees have had to function as if these losses in life did not matter. Many believed that themselves.

When the subject of pain in relinquishment and adoption was discussed on a radio talk show in Phoenix, a caller complained that the topic was even aired. "After all," he said, "my adoption was great and I had no problems forgetting about my birth parents. After all, they forgot about me." Why should this be a problem? Adoptees are loved by their adoptive parents, "more than lots of other kids." But his anger betrayed him. He was far from calm about these opinions. He was deeply invested, as our culture has been, in being sure that relinquishment does not matter. But it does matter.

Ungrieved grief goes somewhere. If, for example, Travis could not have crawled into his mother's arms with his ghost mother hurt, what would have happened? We can only guess what defenses he might have fashioned against those tears, what symptoms might have formed to carry his pain in some way *outside of awareness*. He might have withdrawn into himself to keep the image of his birth mother alive. Or he might have split that image off from his own awareness and denied its meaning to himself. In so doing he would have joined society in believing that there is no pain with which to deal. But "you cannot solve a problem if you say it's not there." Inevitably

Travis would have found a way to present this grief to himself in some fashion. Adoptees, especially in adolescence, may find themselves stealing things like makeup or clothing, the things that mothers buy for children, because they think they deserve that which they have lost. They may be searching for a lost parent. Many adoptees in denial carefully craft the repetition of their own relinquishments in the relationships they form, especially in early adulthood. Others avoid closeness to protect against further hurt. But, one way or another, grief finds a way to be noticed, even after many years. No matter how reasonable it seems to deny the wounds of relinquishment, grief that is not grieved will resurface someday.

Grief that is grieved has rich, although painful, dimensions. Despite the pain of facing such significant losses, adoptees have the opportunity to know themselves more deeply and be known deeply by others because they can learn and tell their birth stories from their hearts. In the words of Paul, they need not grieve as those "who have no hope" (1 Thes. 4:13). Grieving means growing in important ways and coming to terms with reality. This is what each of us must do to be sure of ourselves and to be wise about how we live our lives. Knowing their stories, however painful the stories may be, is liberating in a way that sets adoptees free to truly be themselves. But the knowing does not come without hurting.

Although this chapter presents grieving in terms of the sadness in Travis's tears and Suzanne's heartache, the grieving of relinquishment also involves anger. When we think of anger positively as a protest against an injury, as a sincere expression of self-esteem when the self of an adoptee is under attack, the anger makes sense within the context of grieving. Difficulty arises when angry behavior in a grieving adoptee is punished instead of understood as the awkward expression of pain. When parents punish anger, that may solve their problem in terms of managing a child, but then the child may have difficulty dealing with the reasons for the anger. For example, if an adoptee learns that it is not acceptable to be angry about something, especially something like not knowing your birth parents' whereabouts, then that anger goes "underground," and the seeds are sown for quiet depression.

Grieving also involves struggling with a sense of shame. After all, coming to terms with being relinquished means adoptees accept having birth parents of whom they are not proud. The birth parents' embarrassment about the pregnancy may be internalized in adoptees as being ashamed of themselves, despite the reality that we have no involvement in our own conceptions. One articulate teen adoptee described herself by saying, "I'm just a broken condom!" She was quite clear about her beginnings and found little good in the story. Her comment powerfully portrays the lived experience of some adoptees, who assign such negative value to themselves drawn from their relinquishments. Shame, or negative self-assignment, is a common part of the story of relinquishment and adoption. At times it is so painful that the grieving stops for a while; it gets stuck, because it may be too painful to face having been relinquished, "abandoned to the world."

Grieving includes fear. With uncertainty about the past comes uncertainty about the future. If someone has no sense of a steady foundation in terms of who she or he is, it is understandable that thinking about the future would be frightening rather than exciting. At times this may mean living in fear that "it" will happen again, namely rejection and abandonment. Susan, for example, remembers clearly the day in her teens when her adoptive parents took her to see the Florence Critenton Home for Children in Denver. They may have been joking insensitively when they told her that if she was not good they would send her "back" to such a place, but their words stung Susan because she did indeed fear such a thing. When at the beginning of life a child is "up for grabs," as one adoptee put it, it may set in motion a perpetual fear that the future will always be uncertain. And then fear becomes one of the demons that adoptees must continuously wrestle with in their fight for emotional and spiritual health.

Finally, it may well be that the hallmark of the grieving that adoptees must do is forgiveness. From the perspective of the adoptee, there is a lot to forgive. A middle-aged adoptee named Jim was relinquished but never adopted. He spent his first fourteen years in an orphanage. He remembered both care and abuse in this experience and often wondered why it had to be. At age seven his birth mother paid a visit to his school and announced plans to take him back to live with her and her new husband. But on the day that it was to happen, the stepfather said no to the plan. Jim remembers the schoolmaster telling him the bad news. When Jim asked why, the schoolmaster said he just did not know. Jim walked back to his room, saying to himself, "I guess I am nobody, nobody cares." Fifteen years later his birth mother once again made contact, wanting to see Jim and renew a relationship. At age twenty-two Jim had lunch with her, but then told her he did not want to see her again. This time he was in charge of the relinquishment and he exercised his right to do so. His anger at her and his stepfather had its way. For the next twenty years there was no contact. Jim went on in life without them. But finally his angry heart softened, and he sought them out to tell them that he could now forgive them for what they had done. That forgiveness took twenty years. Jim realized that in order to be free he had to forgive, and this meant reaching deep into his own heart and discovering that, as much as he hated them, he also loved them. Sometimes forgiveness takes a lifetime. It is a process, not a moment, and it is exceedingly difficult if the injury is so primal as relinquishment. But ultimately, forgiveness must happen if the mourning that accompanies relinquishment and adoption is ever to end.

The road of grieving that adoptees walk has many twists and unexpected turns. Only recently has this journey been mapped with any accuracy. Only recently have the twists and turns of grieving been outlined in a manner that makes the trail predictable. In many ways adoptees have been asked to travel blindly, negotiating their way by touch and feel but without the sight of insight. This is now changing, and many adoptees now can avoid some of the potholes in the road, especially if adoptive parents can help their children grieve while they are growing up. But some difficulties must be faced head on and dealt with because there is no way around them. Sometimes the only way is through. The mire of sadness or fires of rage or clouds of shame may slow them down along the way.

But then with more courage, they head onward into their own lives, knowing well that their journeys have been different because they were relinquished. Until recently they have had to do their mourning without anyone's understanding or even their own. They have had to cry and scream and despair on a road kept dark by the laws of the land and innocent ignorance. Now, as our understandings of relinquishment and adoption increase and our empathy for the adoptee's struggles is felt, the road of relinquishment and adoption may be less difficult to walk.

Chapter Three

Adoptee Identity:
The Fruit of Two Trees

It was like I was meeting myself for the first time in twenty-three years. "I know you," I said, as if for the first time I could look in a mirror and see myself.

—*Wendy, age twenty-three*

It was in a cemetery in Michigan that Wendy finally met her birth mother. She has finally "seen" herself in the etchings on the gravestone that marked the place of her birth mother's final rest. Her mother had been dead for five years, having succumbed to breast cancer at age forty-five. Her dying wish, spoken to her sister, was that her birth daughter be found and informed of this important piece of family medical history. Wendy's birth mother wanted her to be checked for lumps in her breasts right away. But it took two years for the adoption agency to make arrangements for the search to proceed so that Wendy could be informed. Word finally came to her, and Wendy remembers both the joy and the sadness of the moment. She was thankful for the medical information. It meant to her that after all these years somehow her birth mother had still cared for her and wanted her to know. However, the news of her birth mother's death hurt deeply. She had now to grieve the loss of the mother that she had never met.

Wendy's adoption was a mixed experience of blessings and difficulties. Her adoptive family had two children by adoption and then two more by birth. Unfortunately, Wendy never felt that she really belonged in this family despite the efforts, especially of her mother, to care for her. She remembers that there always seemed to be a difference between how she was treated and how her siblings by birth were treated during her childhood years. How much of this really came from her adoptive parents and how much of this came from within her is hard to say; nevertheless, her experience growing up seemed to her to be colored by the fact of her relinquishment and adoption. At times the relationship between her and her adoptive father became particularly bad. She recalls "fighting for my own identity" in the face of his expectations about her behavior. For example, Wendy did not want to embrace the conservative moral and political views of her parents. She wanted to enjoy the right to her own more liberal opinion.

When, at age twenty, Wendy married a man of another race, very much against the wishes of her parents, they judged her harshly and held her at a distance, such as by not inviting her to family picnics and other social occasions. Some years later, when she decided after divorce to drop both her married name and family/maiden name and use her middle name as her last name, her adoptive parents ended nearly all communication. She was very much alone in the world, without family, relinquished once again, certainly in part by her own hand.

At age twenty-one, when news came of her birth mother's illness and death, as painful as both were, Wendy felt a sense of excitement about herself, as if somehow she had located an important but missing piece of who she really was. Though she was hesitant about pursuing more information about her birth mother's life and death, her family history, her birth father's story—all of her beginnings—Wendy slowly began to review her life experience, noticing that all along she had kept her distance from people, including her parents, and had never really figured out who she was as a person. Growing up in her adoptive family just didn't work well for her. All along she felt she couldn't be her real self, despite some efforts by her parents and friends to help her develop her own personality. There was something missing. She had tried to make her life work without the missing piece and had been relatively unsuccessful. Her first marriage failed rather quickly. Her attempts in college to define a career did not go far because she did not know what or who she wanted to be. She found herself skipping class and ambivalent about her studies because she felt unsure about where she was headed.

It took nearly two years for Wendy to gather the courage to travel *back* to Michigan to meet her aunt and plan a visit to her birth mother's grave. A new boyfriend went along to give her moral support. She clearly recalls the moment of finding the tombstone with her birth mother's name on it and, in tears, kneeling before it and touching the cold granite that stood like a soldier guarding the grave of what once had been the warm heart of her birth mother, a mother who had never stopped caring and thinking about her.

In a heartfelt letter to Wendy, delivered by her aunt, Wendy's birth mother had stated: "I lived until I was twenty-five, I died when I was forty-five." For twenty years she had existed without living, evidently longing for the connection with Wendy. The story of Wendy's birth, reported by her aunt, was sad. Her birth mother had been in labor for two and a half days

before Wendy was born, as if trying to stop the birth because of the impending loss. She delayed signing the relinquishment papers, trying to find
a way to keep her baby. She was dismayed when the nurses at the hospital
put brown paper bags around the bassinet so that, as Wendy said, "no one
could see me!"

This visit to the cemetery proved to be transformative for Wendy. Finally, she said, she had found herself and her story in the reality of a name
etched in granite.

What does it mean for an adoptee to find herself? What exactly are we
talking about when we address the subject of identity for the adoptee? The
answer has to do with the process of self-definition, of how we all see ourselves in the eyes of others and how we seek to define ourselves before them.
Our identities as persons, our ways of seeing ourselves and presenting ourselves, change from day to day and from moment to moment. We are who
we are depending on where we are and the people with whom we may be.
But there are also certain constants that do not change much despite our
immediate circumstances. These have to do with looks, ethnic background
and heritage, personal history, current interests, likes and dislikes, and values and beliefs. These are all the parts that form us in the sense of making
each of us unique as a human being. *Identity is an ongoing process of self-
definition and self-presentation that has to do with the ebb and flow of these many
variables, some of which are relatively constant and some of which are always
changing.* It is about the experience of a self being a "me."

The person who is relinquished and adopted is uniquely challenged by
the task of identity formation for several reasons. First, the sources from
which one draws one's identity include *both* sets of parents, birth parents
and adoptive parents. But this is not simply in the sense of genetics and environment, as if a descriptive list of characteristics could fill in the missing
pieces that the birth parents provide. Certainly this information is important for the adoptee. But the emotional and spiritual connection to these
people is just as important, even if these ghost parents are only dimly within
the awareness of the adoptee. They are parental figures who form part of
the true self of the adoptee.

A second reason that adoptee identity formation is a unique challenge is
that drawing on two sets of parental figures means dealing with double attachments, with connections that go in two directions. This potential conflict makes it difficult to define oneself without anxiety. At times it has a
negative twist. Researcher Paul M. Brinich explains:

> The tragedies, inabilities, and failures of both the biological and the
> adoptive parents are reflected in the adopted child and his psychological
> development. For the 'realities' of the adult world mean little to the
> young child; the sudden death of loving biological parents may be expe-

rienced as a malicious abandonment; his adoptive parents may tell him that he is 'chosen,' but he may choose to believe he was stolen. No matter how often the adopted child is told that his adoptive parents are not his 'real' parents, he can never completely ignore his first parents and the fact that they gave him up.[1]

For the adoptee, who *is* from two sets of parents, the stage is set at the beginning of life for ongoing inner difficulty. And loyalty to one parent or set of parents may be experienced as disloyalty or even disconnection from another. This psychic bind means that the process of identity formation becomes complicated for adoptees; in fact they may quite understandably hesitate to engage in this task.

The Bedrock of Identity

It may well be that the knowledge that we were conceived in love is the foundation for personal self-esteem, a sense of self that is experienced as positive and valued, as if we really matter. The idea that our very beginning, the moment of our conception, occurred within a context of deep love and commitment between our parents may ground us in a sense of our own personal importance. Object-relations theorist D. W. Winnicott makes this point:

> The sexual union of father and mother provides a fact, a hard fact around which the child may build a fantasy, a rock to which he can cling and against which he can kick; and furthermore it provides part of the natural foundation for a personal solution to the problem of the triangular [Oedipal] relationship.[2]

Conversely, what might the adoptee count on as a bedrock truth about himself in terms of his beginning? What might it mean to learn that your conception as a person was accidental between two people unable, for whatever reason, to commit to each other, who indeed may not have been very much in love with each other? How might one deal with the knowledge of being unplanned, unwanted, an accident in time? How might this affect the development of self?

"I'm Just a Broken Condom!"

Patty, for example, was a sixteen-year-old adoptee who had difficulties all along growing up in her adoptive home. Her adoptive mother put considerable effort into spending time with her, making connection as best she could, and taking the initiative to raise the issues of concern that surround relinquishment and adoption. But, for some reason, Patty could not hear her adoptive mother's offer to care.

In her adolescence Patty became intensely oppositional. She ran away several times, heading for the streets upon which she imagined her birth mother lived. She smoked marijuana and quit her high school studies. Her protest against her own life left her, at times, in a suicidal state of mind. And then, in a moment of deeply felt confrontation with both her adoptive parents and herself she screamed to her mother that she was just a "broken condom." In contrast to being the result of two people's deep love and commitment to each other and to her future, she knew well that she was unplanned. Patty did not have the benefit of seeing herself in her very beginning as someone with value. Instead she saw herself, and treated herself, as a broken condom, an accident, some *thing* to be discarded.

Patty dropped out of high school, smoked more marijuana, and became involved in an abusive relationship following this profound moment of truth. When she screamed those painful words of self-depreciation, she expressed a core truth adoptees sometimes keep secretly in their hearts—that their value as a person feels optional, that from the moment of their beginning they were "up for grabs." Who would want to start life being up for grabs?

Stern's Idea of an Early Self

In order to be a self, a person must have some sense of his own experience. This may or may not be at a conscious level, but it needs to somehow *be* there, even in a primitive way, for the development of a self to proceed. More traditional theory about self-development has suggested that the dawning of self-awareness for infants occurs as they begin to take leave from their primary caregiver, an initially symbiotic relationship. As separation begins, a sense of self emerges. Developmental theorist Margaret Mahler,[3] for example, suggests that this sense of self begins at fifteen to eighteen months of age.

Obviously the implications of such a way of thinking about development relate directly to the possible implications of relinquishment and adoption at an early age. *The degree to which relinquishment is traumatic and the degree to which adoption may be compromised depend directly on the capacity of the infant-child to be an experiencing self.* If, as people like Mahler and attachment theorist M.D.S. Ainsworth[4] have suggested, this ability does not really develop until a child is over a year old, then it is certainly questionable how much an experience of self exists and, accordingly, how much psychic pain occurs in the sense of loss.

Daniel N. Stern, an infant psychiatrist, sees it differently. He bases his theory about the early development of the self on observational studies of infants and young children. He suggests that traditional thinking about an emerging sense of the self is based more on adults' reconstructive analyses than on actual observation of children, and that the former simply does not hold up as valid under scrutiny. In contrast to a "later view," Stern suggests that the self of the infant is there from early on, that differentiation begins almost at birth and continues in a four-step process involving more complex ways of relatedness. If this is true, it follows that the very young adoptee may be aware of the *experience* of relinquishment and adoption and be hurt. Stern cites, for example, a study of three-day-old infants lying on their backs with breast pads filled with milk from their mothers on one side and milk from other mothers on the other side. He notes how the infants "reliably turned their heads towards their own mothers' pads, regardless of which side the pads were on."[5] They could sense the smell of their own mother's milk. They knew. He writes:

> Infants begin to experience a sense of an emergent self from birth. They are predesigned to be aware of self-organizing processes. They never experience a period of total self/other undifferentiation. There is no confusion between self and other at the beginning or at any point during infancy.[6]

Stern argues that the sense of being a self is the primary organizing principle of development.[7] He suggests a developmental progression that begins with the "emergent self" and spans the period between birth and two months of age. This is the neonate as she gazes differently at live faces or discriminates her mother's voice from that of others. This is about the beginning of a sense of self in the earliest days of life, which entails the capacity to *experience*, if even in a very primitive way.

From two months to six months, according to Stern, infants are more integrated in social situations than previously thought, and they develop what he calls a "core sense of self." In this phase, the world of interpersonal relationships is very much in place as the infant employs this core self in relating to others. The self-experiences that Sterns notes at this age include self-agency (having an awareness of control over one's own behavior and not over that of others), self-coherence (a sense of physical wholeness and boundary between self and others), self-affectivity (experiencing the inner quality of feelings), and self-history (a sense of continuity with the past that "goes on being," a Winnicottian idea). Based on a sense of self *and* other comes a sense of self *with* other, all within the first six months of life. And, of course, if relinquishment and adoption occur within these first few months of life, then the changes in caregiving are *experienced* by the child, who is an experiencing self and aware of the impingements on development that may result. This is "the muddling of the environment"[8] in which the adoptee must develop.

Stern goes on to suggest that between seven and fifteen months the sense of a "subjective self" develops, in which the infant realizes that a framework of meaning and communication can be shared with others. Interpersonal relatedness switches from demonstrating overt behaviors to demonstrating underlying subjective states of experience. The infant shows feelings and the ability to share an affective state with another. This is the beginning of psychic intimacy, the awareness of connection as a subjective self.

With the development of language comes Stern's fourth category of self-development, the "verbal self." Words permit the infant to create and share more mutual experiences. The world of symbolic play opens up for children as they acquire the use of language and define themselves more objectively within relationships with others. They look in the mirror with new curiosity about themselves and begin to name their experience and themselves as distinct persons. They *know* who they are very early in life.

According to Stern, the relinquished and adopted child may, in the course of development, experience what he calls "primitive agonies" about "*actual* disruptions"[9] that occur in the exchange of parents. To the degree that the infant-child is an experiencing self, who makes an appraisal both cognitively and emotionally of the loss of birth parents and the new "dance of connection" with adoptive parents, the relinquished and adopted infant is challenged to make sense of the experience, mourn the loss involved, and define himself in the midst of a new and confusing environment. For adoptees to "come of age" as very young persons is to face varying degrees of initial "non-attunement" with adoptive parents where there are differing degrees of "unsharability of subjective experience."[10] Simply put, the self of the relinquished and adopted child may well be aware of what is going on, and then must manage this change in life experience as much as possible, but with limited resources to do so. To whatever degree this is *experienced* as an overwhelming task, attachment to new parents and new people may necessarily be compromised. An early self, as it is based on Stern's observations and theory, means more awareness on adoptees' part of their task of managing change in caregivers. This means more work to do in terms of becoming a person.

Primary Identifications

Some years ago I found myself busy in our garage changing the oil in an old Ford Maverick. As I was walking from one corner of the garage to another, retrieving several quarts of oil for the task, I noticed our then three-year-old son with a quart of oil stepping along behind me. Then I heard words that I have never forgotten. "I want to help, Dad, I want to be like you."

Children usually seek to internalize their parents, at least initially, in the early years of development. Our son was looking for a way to be. For several years thereafter he was my "oilman," always ready to help with the job that came around every three thousand miles or so. As his father, I was one of his primary sources of identity. Something important was going on in the garage in terms of his development as a self, a person with certain unique characteristics. Being able to carry a quart of oil to the car meant being a boy who knew about oil changes and who could help to make them happen. This little piece of information defined him. It was both a given, because I, his father, was an oil changer, and an intentional act in terms of his self-presentation, because he too wanted to be an oil changer. He was drawing from the wonderful chaos of his early experience to form his sense of person. Someday he would be an oil changer without my help because that was his early wish.

From the countless experiences that each of us has in our years of growing up we gather bits and pieces to create our own identities. In a sense, we manufacture ourselves and form a sturdy sense of the *who* that each of us is. And this identity gives each of us a sense of security about our "continuity of being" into the future. The person, for example, who states that she doesn't know who she is most often speaks these difficult words feeling depressed or having difficulty finding direction. Clarity about one's identity makes for smoother sailing in life. But for the relinquished and adopted person, such clarity is hard to come by because some of the primary sources of identity may be unavailable for useful internalization.

Paul Brinich, in "Some Potential Effects of Adoption on Self and Object Representations,"[11] describes the adoptee's difficulty in terms of putting things and people together.

> Every child uses a combination of personal experiences, cultural materials, and constitutional givens to create mental representations of himself and of people and the world around him. These mental representations are organized into a 'representational world' used by the child to predict the outcome of his interactions with people and with the world. Thus, the child's mental representations of himself and others influence his object relationships. The adopted child must include two separate sets of parents within his representational world. He must also integrate into his representation of himself the fact that he was born to one set of parents but has been raised by another set of parents.[12]

The relinquished and adopted child is, accordingly, faced with the dilemma of drawing from four parents—parental representations—in the formation of his identity. But, given that birth parents are for the most part hidden figures in the story, it becomes difficult if not impossible to "put oneself together." This is what Wellisch in the 1950s first called "genealogical bewilderment,"[13] by which he meant that adoptees (in the world of the closed adoption system) are, of necessity, left with unknowns about their birth parents, personal history, ethnic and cultural heritage, and birth and relinquishment stories—all missing and important parts of their backgrounds. The resulting experience of confusion and uncertainty makes identity formation especially difficult. How can one accomplish the task of self-determination without access to all the pieces of the puzzle?

Birth Parents—Important Pieces of the Puzzle

The question "Who am I?" can be answered in so many ways. When little is known about the reality of the birth parents, adoptees are left to wonder, to speculate about those ghost parents who hold the truth to an important part of their stories. First of all, there are the unknown basics. Adoptees in the closed adoption system may not know their own nationalities. For them ethnic jokes are not funny because they cannot identify with them. They may not know the reason they were relinquished; often an adoptee is told only that "she loved you so much she decided to do this for you." Few adoptees really see how love and abandonment could fit together. Instead they may quietly think, "If she loved me more, she would have found a way to keep me!"

Relinquished and adopted persons are left to wonder, mostly by way of fantasy (the subject of chapter 5). Sometimes they wonder in a positive way, but many imagine their birth parents in a negative light. After all, birth parents are portrayed as people unable or unwilling to do whatever it takes to keep a child. Birth mothers are often thought of as promiscuous and uncaring, since they did become pregnant and did relinquish. Birth fathers are often thought of as irresponsible men who disappear when the news of pregnancy is told. And so, as development proceeds, negative images become the basis of birth parent identifications, and these images form part of the adoptee's identity. For children growing up with their own by-birth parents who care in a reasonable way, there are positive images, such as exciting stories about the day of a child's birth. But for the adoptee, often negative images—stories of shame rather than of pride—become the first chapter of life. And when shame and embarrassment are shrouded in secrecy, in the closed files of the courtroom or the silence of the adoptive home, then the adoptee is left with little but negative fragments of a painful relinquishment out of which to construct a personal history, the foundation of personal identity.

For many years the thinking behind the secrecy about relinquishment and adoption included the idea of protecting adoptees from the shame of their stories and knowledge of the "bad seed" of their origins. A falsified birth certificate was thought to be a better option that one that was true but stamped "bastard child." In the early part of this century, such thinking guided adoption agencies and the social workers involved for decades, and relinquishment and adoption records were closed. The down side to all this secrecy, however, was the continuing reinforcement of the shame of the story.

Carol was placed for adoption in a state home in North Dakota. She had a medical condition that required extensive surgery and nearly a year of recovery before foster parents began her care. The legal document that she eventually retrieved stated that she had been "abandoned to the world" and was therefore adoptable by new parents. At age three she was at last adopted, and she grew up on a farm with several adopted siblings. But all along she wondered, as many adoptees do, why she had been "given up." Was it because of her heart condition? Did her birth parents even know about it? Was it because she cried too much? Her questions and fantasy answers about her relinquishment were part of development as she grew up on the farm, wondering. She learned to hide from people, to keep her distance. Certainly that was in part because her life began with several difficult interruptions in care, but *in her words* it was more because she was not worth much; that she did not carry much value as a person. She felt defective and thrown away in the beginning, and had internalized this belief about herself. She did not see people as a resource. She had never dated much or married, but instead stayed safe and alone. It was a negative puzzle piece from her birth parents that she had taken to heart. In her mind they were not much and neither was she.

How many positive or negative images do adoptees "get" from birth parents as pieces for the puzzle of identity? Should they be proud of a birth father who was an athlete or of a birth mother who did well in school? Or should they be ashamed of a birth mother who was a prostitute or a birth father who fled the scene? If parents are primary sources of identity, as well as self-esteem, and if adoptees are faced with little information about birth parents except the negative fragments of information that often accompany a relinquishment story, then we can understand why adoptees face serious struggles in identity formation. We know this before we even consider the contribution that adoptive parents can make toward a solid sense of who adoptees might *be*. The relinquished and adopted person who manages this developmental task well deserves all the more credit for doing something more difficult than those of us in the nonadoptive world will ever know. It is indeed a challenge to be an adopted *person*.

Adoptive Parents—
The Other Important Pieces of the Puzzle

Adoptive parents almost always approach their children with the best of intentions. The fundamental security that is absolutely necessary for healthy human development is certainly at stake at the beginning of this family formation. And, as with any parents, adoptive parents have so much to offer to assure that a child can grow up well. There are thousands of moments of experience to make use of as building blocks for the formation of a person. Being held, being seen, and being cared for in all the ordinary ways of mothering and fathering from the day of birth, if possible, and onward are the needed pieces for development . . . *if* the child allows the care and takes in the blessing of it.

The first challenge that adoptees face, and one that is most often a surprise and secret disappointment to their adoptive parents, has to do with the initial bonding and ongoing attachment to these new parents. If it goes well, then the strength that this connection provides will allow for the many internalizations to occur which will translate into a secure sense of a personal identity for the adoptee. But if not, then despite the consistent efforts of adoptive parents to get into the hearts of their children, the adoptee may "take in" these new people only in a limited way. And this, of course, means that the child's sense of identity will be more fragile, as with the adoptees who report that, despite the efforts of their adoptive parents to enhance the connections, they never felt as if they really *belonged* in their adoptive families. This may be especially true if there is a blend of children by adoption and children by birth. Therefore, adoptees and adoptive parents may be at a disadvantage from the beginning in terms of bonding and attachment. If so, then the process of identity formation for the relinquished and adopted child may be incomplete, compromised by difficulties in trusting the new arrangement of the adoptive family.

Another challenge that the adoptee may face in terms of identity formation involves issues that the adoptive parents themselves must address. It is a delicate line that each of us walks between becoming ourselves, as we think and want ourselves to be, and becoming what our parents want us to be, given their ideas about our lives and their values for our lives. When adoptive parents deal well with the issues of their own lives, especially infertility and the grief that accompanies it, then adopted children have "free space" in which to become themselves, *whatever* that might be. The adoptive parents then have the freedom to *discover* their children as well as form them. But like most human beings, adoptive parents carry their own unique dynamic of difficulties with life, and inevitably their stories get caught up in the development of their children. For the adoptee these dynamics may be especially complex.

Ken came for pastoral counseling at the age of twenty-one. He had made several attempts at going to school but found nothing that excited him. To avoid failing he had dropped out twice. He was alone and feeling aimless. His parents were both overseas, where his father was employed as an oil executive. Ken had grown up in a highly competitive home as an adoptee with an older sibling born to this family. When conception was no longer a possibility for medical reasons, his parents made a plan for adoption. In his own words, "It was never a match." He recalled the many instances of his parents celebrating his older brother's accomplishments. This brother was a star athlete in football, basketball, and baseball—all three! Ken remembers how he felt going to these games and noticing his father's pride in the touchdown passes, three-point shots, and homerun hits over the fence. But Ken was unathletic. He felt diminished and invisible. Despite earlier efforts to follow in those footsteps and emulate his brother's success, Ken realized that he was a different person. He was built differently and not coordinated as an athlete needs to be. Ken struggled to find his way without the sense of being a son that his parents were proud of. He loved music, and at the time of his counseling he was playing bass guitar in a band with friends. This seemed to "work" for him. At least for the time being. He enjoyed their evening practices held in somebody's garage. He reported that he was still trying to figure out who he wanted to be, and that thus far his efforts were getting him nowhere. His parents subsidized his living expenses so there was no great need to work more than his part-time church janitor job demanded. Ken was free to be, but could not find a way to his being.

After several weeks of pastoral counseling Ken became more animated as he described the plans that he and his music-making friends were making for their future as a band. Although he would earn little money, he stated his commitment to stay with this for a while. He was well aware of his parents' not-so-subtle disappointment with him. His older brother was doing well as a teacher-coach at a local high school. But, in the eyes of his parents and also in his own eyes, his life was not working.

In counseling there was talk about relinquishment and adoption and further conversation about the less-than-his-brother dynamic in the family. Ken knew that his birth mother loved music. He was not sure if that bit of "non-identifying information" meant that she was a musician or simply a person who enjoyed listening, but he did know and he did say, "Well, she would be proud of me."

The relinquished and adopted person has *two* sets of parents that have much to do with the formation of the person. For Ken the internalizations of his birth mother's pleasure in his music and his adoptive father's disappointment in his life served as key components in his current self-definition. The dynamic that was playing out in his life, at this time, included a lot of anger at parents whose "be like me" messages put him in an impossible bind. This young man was not an athlete. He could not please the caregiver. Marijuana spelled relief. And, on the other, secret side of his story, the single fantasy that his birth mother would be proud of him gave him energy to keep on going. He left counseling after only seven sessions, not appearing for the last. Connecting was especially difficult. There was more to do in terms of determining his sense of self before he could deal with some of the pain about the initial loss of his birthright and the ongoing difficulties of nonattunement in his adoptive family. He left with some awareness of where some of his answers would be found. Some of these answers might be treasures, some stones, but either way, they were the truth about who Ken was, which would allow Ken to *be* somebody.

One adoptive parent puzzle piece that often plays in development for relinquished and adopted children has to do with overprotectiveness by their parents. When parents are "given" a child, sometimes they respond with a variety of understandable but uncomfortable feelings. They may first feel guilty that they have somehow stolen a child, regardless of reality. This sense of something being wrong may lead to their feeling a *lack* of entitlement to truly being the child's parents. If so, then the parents may constantly feel the need to prove their parenthood, and may indulge their children with more than is wise in terms of care and of things. Or adoptive parents may move from the guilt about adoption to fearful overprotectiveness, believing, if only in fantasy, that because this child is not *really* theirs, that the birth mother and maybe birth father may return to take the child back. This makes for overprotective impulses that inevitably teach the adopted child that the world is not a safe place to be. It is a part of adoptive *parent* development with which relinquished and adopted children have to cope.

On a rather delightful summer afternoon two adoptees clamored for Mom to take them swimming at the community pool down the street. Mom said yes, though not without a nervous twitch in her voice. She knew it was a reasonable request. The hot sun was beating down on everyone in Dallas and the pool certainly seemed to be the right place to be. Friends were there for the children, and other mothers sat with iced tea in hand, talking the afternoon away, thankful to be with a few adults amidst the chatter of boys and girls. And it was safe: experienced lifeguards sat on each side of the pool, alert and scanning the scene for possible trouble. And both children, ages seven and ten, were taking swimming lessons. But Sally, the adoptive mom, could not relax. Though it all looked so safe, Sally was afraid every time they went to the pool. She feared that one of the children would drown, despite all the safety measures in place. She knew it was "irrational." She had discussed it many times with her husband. But the fear did not go away. She was afraid and she was teaching her children to be afraid. She did not like this but she could not stop it.

Sally was afraid that somehow something bad would happen to her children and she might lose one. There was no way to relax and enjoy the company of neighbors. Not until they left the pool and headed home could she calm down. So much appeared to be at stake. She could not lose again. In her struggles with infertility she had already lost, well before these children came to her and her husband by adoption. Further loss may have seemed incomprehensible, an ordeal too awful to consider. Neither lifeguards nor life vests could quell the storm of fear inside her. And, unfortunately, her children were learning that the world they were trying to enjoy was not a safe place. Instead, it was to be feared and avoided. There could be no real fun at the pool with Mom sitting on the edge reminding them to be careful. Sometimes growing up with adoptive parents means figuring out a way to take care of *them*.

Secondary Sources of Adoptee Identity

Adoptees draw on sources other than birth and adoptive parents to create their identities. These other sources deserve comment because they are especially meaningful to many adoptees in ways that those of us who are not relinquished and adopted may not immediately appreciate. Of the many points of reference that adoptees employ in the formation of self, the following play a special role.

Culture

Kate came from Korea. She was relinquished by her birth father at age eighteen months and placed in an orphanage in Seoul. Her birth mother history is not known. At three and a half she was adopted by an Anglo family in America and grew up as best she could in a white world. Her early disruptions in attachment caused significant difficulties with trusting others and allowing for closeness in her life, including closeness with both of her adoptive parents. She reported that they made considerable effort to be available and to make a connection with her. But, despite all their efforts, she remembers feeling like a stranger in her own home. Her age at adoption would certainly account for many of these difficulties, but she reported that there was always an important *cultural* issue as well. She was not Anglo on the inside or the outside, and she recalled often wondering what she really was. Unfortunately, Korean was just a word to her, a connection to something lost. But what it was she did not know beyond the story told of her orphanage experience. Trace memories reminded her of its truth, but it felt like a vague mystery to her. What did it mean to her to be Korean? How could she be Korean in America, growing up in an Anglo family? Cultural background is not just history, it defines a *person*.

In Korea the tiger is regarded with immense respect as a creature with cunning and wisdom. The Korean culture sets the tiger apart from other animals and considers it unique because of its strength, beauty, and intelligence. Kate learned of this veneration of the tiger in Korean culture, and when she was in college she got a tattoo of a tiger on her lower left leg. The tattoo identified her, making clear to her who she was in the midst of America. She experienced this as a way to reclaim a part of who she was and wanted to be. When asked about the tattoo, she had an opportunity to explain a bit about the land in which she was born. With some pride she could tell of the role of the tiger in Korean culture. In her own words, her identity was "more in place."

"Cultural loss" is an obvious issue in cases of international and cross-cultural adoptions where the differences between the adoptee and the adoptive parents are obvious to the eye. When children come to an American family from Korea, China, Romania, or other foreign countries, the loss of cultural heritage is clear, and adoptive parents can do much to "keep" the child's culture in the home by teaching of that culture, respecting cultural practices and dress, or simply decorating their home in a way that connects the child to its homeland. But, nevertheless, the loss is obvious and real. Where differences are less than obvious, where relinquished and adopted children look enough like their parents that others only wonder about adoption, there may still be *for the adoptee* the experience of loss of culture. Here the term "culture" may be used more broadly to define the world that a given birth parent creates and lives in. For example, an adoptee who found his birth mother and six half siblings in Minneapolis reported with surprise that "they all listen to Rush Limbaugh!" Although he was a Democrat by life experience, he evidently was not one by birth. The culture of his birth mother, and perhaps birth father, was foreign to him, something that he had lost. The adoptee may always wonder, "Who would I be if I had been brought up in the land and in the family that began me?" This question of the would-have-been person complicates the identity formation of the adoptee because, not only are there the missing cultural components with which to deal, but there are also the wonderings of who a person would be if he had been raised by his family of origin. And, once again, the adoptee is challenged to make a *person* out of the pieces that are left in a new culture with its new beliefs and values and traditions.

A Name

In Isaiah 45 God says to the people of Israel,

> For the sake of Jacob my servant,
>   of Israel my chosen,
> I summon you by name
>   and bestow on you a title of honor.—Verse 4

There is a lot in a name, especially for adoptees. When, for example, a child says she does not like her name, this may be a clue to some struggles with low self-esteem. When an adoptee's name is changed from one given by a birth parent to one given by adoptive parents, the *idea* of such a change is sometimes experienced as a blow of some sort. This cognitive awareness, of course, comes along in early latency when children figure these things out. The point is that a name has meaning. It is not simply a person's label or tag of some sort. It *is* that person. A name is identity. For this reason relinquished and adopted persons may express interest in the name given on their original birth certificates and feel a sense of disappointment if only "boy Smith" is written there.

Because names are such an obvious source of identity, it should be no surprise that adoptees take them seriously. When Kate, described above, learned that her given name at the Korean orphanage was Kimjin, she took this as her middle name, introducing herself as Kathryn Kimjin. For her it was a more complete statement of who she really was. Her middle name gave her more of a sense of her identity, both in terms of who she was and who she wanted to be. Sometimes the adoptee does not want to offend adoptive parents, and therefore decisions like Kate's occur only in adulthood or after adoptive parents are gone. It is not uncommon for relinquished and adopted adults who are struggling with issues of personal identity to make changes in their names to reflect who they are and want to be. Erik Erikson, for example, literally renamed himself as Erik the son of Erik when he came to America. He learned at age sixteen that his birth father was not the noted pediatrician, Theodor Homburger, with whom he had grown up. This experience was a significant injury. As a child and as an adolescent he often wondered why he was so tall and blond, so Scandinavian, while his German "father" was so dark and short. No wonder that he has had so much to say about identity and the problems involved. He understood the struggle in a firsthand way. His renaming of himself was his way to resolve some of the identity conflict that the news of his true birth father set in motion.[14] In a most unusual way adoptees are challenged to *create* themselves, drawing on the identities of their adoptive families while also drawing on their knowledge of the names from which they came and the names that they were given. Their names matter because names are people, and adoptees, like the rest of us, desire to be people in the fullest sense of the word.

Birth Siblings

We mainly think of the role of birth *parents* in an adoptee's experience of identity formation from the birth side of the story, and these parents obviously play a significant role in determining identity. However, there is also the possibility that half or full siblings exist who may assist in the formation and completion of the adoptee's identity.

John, for example, grew up as an only child in his adoptive home. He remembers wishing often that he had a sibling, someone to play with or fight with and simply be with. Being a brother, in his own words, was always something that was missing for him. At age fifty he learned, in search and reunion, that indeed he had several half siblings, one of whom lived within sixty miles of his home. Her name was Karen. Upon meeting her he discovered that the experience of being a brother overwhelmed him. All his life he had wanted this and now, in finding his half sister, he had found what he called a "much stronger sense of self." It was as if a part of *him* which had been missing was found. Adoptees who find birth siblings in search and reunion often report that learning about being someone's sister or brother changes how they view themselves, even if the relationships don't go well. Part of the formation and completion of the adoptee self may include the news of being a sibling and therefore *related* to someone. Part of being a person includes the connections that we may have with others with whom we share both cultural and genetic history. Siblings are part of that story.

Medical Information

Adoptees who are hesitant about the idea of search and possible reunion with birth parents still express an interest in knowing their medical history. Sometimes the nonidentifying information that agencies allow the adoptee may contain some data about medical background, but usually it does not. Here again relinquished and adopted people are left to wonder about basic physical and medical facts about themselves. There are, of course, practical reasons for wanting to know medical history. With the ever-increasing body of knowledge available today about hundreds of diseases and medical conditions that are genetic in origin and better treated with early detection and diagnosis, it is obvious that adoptees have good reason, as well as the human right, to know their medical pedigrees. It can literally be a matter of life and death.

For example, a birth mother was recently diagnosed with chronic active autoimmune hepatitis, a genetic disorder. She learned that she may have ten more years to live but that this disease will progressively destroy body functions. She now wants very much to inform her birth son that he may be carrying this condition and may need to prepare for its onset. This knowledge, as difficult as it may be, is something he has a right to know and a need to know in terms of planning and treatment. He is, as has been said, "at medical disadvantage" if he does not know.

But there is more to be said about knowledge of birth parents' medical history for the adoptee. It is not just a medical issue. It is also an identity issue. This information is part of the *who* that a person is. Although hesitant adoptees sometimes say that they are only interested in their medical histories for reasons of health and fitness, at a deeper level they may be seeking to further define themselves without acknowledging that they are doing so. Even negative information about health history is still information that serves as a source of identity for the relinquished person. "I come from a history of heart disease" is a statement that is not only about the need to attend to the possibility of heart problems but also a piece of the puzzle of identity, a way of knowing something more about lost birth parents. This is also a matter of the heart. Medical information may serve a double benefit for adoptees. Certainly it helps in terms of adequate health care and planning, but it also gives further definition to the person of the adoptee, a connection to the birth history and story of the identity of birth parents. It is another way to know about *oneself*.

Adoptee Adolescence

Kristin, at age sixteen, was handed the child to whom she had just given birth. When she saw her daughter for the first time, she exclaimed, "For the first time in my life I have someone who looks like me!" At the risk of adding a special stigma for female adoptees to the stigma that all adoptees may face, the question here is not so much about the incidence but about the *meaning* of a teenage adoptee becoming pregnant.

Especially in adolescence, the question of identity comes to the front stage of development. Teenagers wonder about both who they are and who they want to be. Their task in this wondrous, crazy, sometimes painful, stage of life is to define themselves in such a fashion that each teen becomes the person that he or she can live with. This is to say that a part of the struggle of adolescence is to build a personal identity that is satisfying, with which one can be happy. This is the difficult but lifelong important work of self-definition. So when a teen decides to put a ring in his ear or her navel, it is not simply a matter of looking for someone's attention, especially that of an anxious parent. It is first a matter of presenting oneself to the world as a unique individual who has a need to be seen and understood in a certain fashion. Well, how might a pregnancy be part of the story for an adoptee in a way that is different from that of her nonadopted peers?

Much has been written about the struggles of relinquished and adopted adolescents.[15] There is little question that adolescence is an unusually difficult time for adoptees. Their over-representation in the clinical population across the country indicates that something is especially difficult for them at this particular time in life. But should this be a surprise? *The adoptee is asked to face the challenge of identity formation without all the pieces needed to do so.* Identity formation involves both learning about who you are from history and from lived experience and deciding who you are when confronted with choices in everyday life. Relinquished and adopted adolescents are clearly at a disadvantage in terms of the demand to piece together who they are if they do not know much about the ghost parents who *are* part of the story.

Lifton writes in a chapter entitled "Good Adoptee-Bad Adoptee"[16] about the way many relinquished and adopted children adapt to their role in the "adoption game" by going in one of two directions. In the first case, as a "good adoptee," the child or adolescent adapts carefully to the expectations of adoptive parents as a defense against the horrible possibility of further relinquishment. It is important to note that this adaption of good behavior is different from the task of being good because of solid and clear attachment. Instead, it is meant to be protective and so it is *experienced* differently, as an "as-if" persona that protects the true self from injury. This adaption is usually a matter of degree. But it is an important distinction, because, if good behavior and a good identity are not experienced as connected with the true self of the adoptee, sooner or later the adaption will wear out or lead to depression of some sort.

For Lifton the "good adoptee" secures the future, defending successfully against more rejection by always doing the right thing and working hard to please everybody around. This is the child who may sail through adolescence but never really experience adolescence in terms of forming a real and true self.

Or, sometimes like time bombs, good adoptees find the *courage* to shift, to step away from goodness enough to let their families know that they are struggling. They act out, they scream that everything is not OK. They communicate by their behavior that they are in pain and that they need help with it, an understandable but difficult and risky thing to do. Becoming a "bad adoptee" in adolescence means taking on the fears of further abandonment that may have haunted the adoptee all along. If the risk is too great to take, it may never occur, leaving the adoptee feeling like a partial person, or it will only occur when the risk is lower, often in midlife when the variables of risk and relationship have changed.

Other adoptees, according to Lifton, start out as "bad adoptees" and do not allow the closeness and comfort that being "good" would facilitate. These are the difficult children and adolescents who prefer to fight, to stay away, to act out in defiance—all as a way to communicate their struggles with closeness and with taking the risk of being cared for deeply. This, for example, may explain the teenage adoptee who gets pregnant, who does the "wrong thing" to deal with her relinquished and adopted dilemma. *Becoming* her birth mother by becoming pregnant cements the tie, the powerful identification, with the person who gave *her* birth. Finding someone "who looks like me" affirms the sense of self that she may be struggling to find. And keeping the baby may be her way to "correct" the pain of her own relinquishment. Making a plan for adoption may be recapitulating her central life dilemma with or without finding the resolution that she needs to heal from the hurt of her own relinquishment.

Being the "bad adoptee" offers the adopted teen a method to communicate the pain of the catch-22 of relinquishment and adoption. Lifton writes,

> The Bad Adoptees are the ones who cannot adequately repress their sense of lack of connection. They cannot tolerate it. They act out as a way of feeling alive. To prove that they exist. *He* goes in for stealing, setting fires, smashing up the family car, taking drugs, and running away. *She* may pop pills, steal, or run away, but she also acts out sexually by becoming pregnant.[17]

No wonder that being an adopted teen is especially difficult. Whether by way of repressing, as the "good adoptee" does, or by acting out, as the "bad adoptee" does, the major task of adolescence—to form a cohesive and comfortable identity—is complicated by the reality of relinquishment and the struggle to allow adoptive parents to be the resources that they can be.

The relinquished and adopted teen who (1) successfully navigates adolescence by drawing on the strengths of all *four* of his parents as best he can, (2) sorts out his own experience of dislikes with all *four* of his parents, (3) accepts the strengths and weaknesses of all of them, and (4) accepts the self that this makes him, at least enough to get along in everyday life, has accomplished a Herculean feat. These relinquished and adopted teens are those who have "adjusted" to the circumstances and realities of their different lives—different because they were relinquished and adopted. However, many other adoptees have more difficulties. When, because of our society's secrecy about ghost parents, teenage adoptees do *not* think about their birth parent stories and when they attempt to navigate adolescence *without* the benefit of bringing their birth parents into focus, then they are especially at risk in terms of derailing, of crashing, and of needing extra help getting their wheels back on track. They do adjust. To their credit, most do get back on track. Adoptees are *not* over-represented in the adult clinical populations across our country. They are people who have become themselves, difficult as that may be.

The Role of Search and Reunion

Until recently an adoptee's desire to search for his birth parents was thought to be a symptom of poor attachment to his adoptive parents. It was believed that if the relationship between the relinquished and adopted child and his parents was adequate, there would be no need for such a quest. Love from adoptive parents should be enough. *Needing* to locate one's birth parents and form a relationship with them was seen as pathological, as something that the adoptee needed help with, to work through, and to *relinquish*. More recent literature suggests a different view of search and reunion efforts.[18] Finding what was lost, despite the obvious effects of time on these connections, is seen as potentially useful.

In terms of the concerns of this chapter on identity, much can be said for this usefulness. *The more one knows, the less one guesses.* For relinquished and adopted children who are now growing up in the context of more open adoptions, much more information is available to them and their parents about the birth parents. When simple questions can be answered about who one's birth parents are, where they live, how they live, what they are doing and all the rest, then obviously there is more reality in which to ground one's development of identity. And, accordingly, there is less need to construct fantasies about birth parents, fantasies that may serve the purpose of keeping connection (the subject of chapter 5). But not knowing means wondering. For adolescent adoptees, who in the course of normal development struggle if they don't know about their ghost parents, being more informed about the birth parents would mean less difficulty in putting together the pieces of self. Today more teens and young adults are pursuing search and reunion because they feel the need to do so. Adoptive parents and society are increasingly allowing them to do so. Carl (described in chapter 1), for example, made indirect contact with Patty, his birth mother, when he was eleven in order to both grieve the losses of his given reality and to move toward the identity struggles of his adolescent years. And now many young and middle-aged adults pursue search and reunion to continue their adult development and bring to rest the many questions and emotions that have been an ongoing part of their daily lives.

Roger was one such adult. Though as a child he often wondered about his birth mother, he never felt allowed to ask about her. As a child he discovered that it was not acceptable to talk about his relinquishment and, as a "good adoptee," he didn't. His life proceeded in an ordinary way with friends, a good education, and what looked like a good life as a youth minister in a large California congregation—until he faced the sudden and bitter end of his three-year marriage because, as his wife put it, "You never let me love you, you insisted that I didn't, and that was that!" The painful upheaval of divorce was the ticket that brought Roger to his emotional knees and to the counselor's door. The search began in earnest that had always been in fantasy.

"All adoptees engage in a search process," report the authors of a study of nearly one hundred adoptees whom they interviewed. "[I]n our experience . . . it may not be a literal search, but it is meaningful nonetheless. It begins when the child first asks, 'Why did it happen?' 'Who are they?' 'Where are they now?'"[19] Their point is that *all* adoptees pursue a psychic search of some kind in their development. Now Roger was making his a real search. There was the usual red tape, with the adoption agency giving him as little as possible of the information to which he believed he had a human right. There were roadblocks in the way because he had no name with which to start. It took years of checking hospital records with his date of birth, finding possibilities, scanning high school yearbooks, and checking the Internet for names and locations. Finally, Roger learned, after believing that he had located his birth mother, that both of his birth parents had died several years before his search began, which was not much satisfaction for all his effort. But still he boarded a plane to Wisconsin to visit the aunt he had thought at first was his mother and then to visit the cemetery where his birth mother was buried. It was a sad and painful ending to his quest.

But it was also a beginning. With a picture of her in hand he kissed the gravestone, which, in his words, seemed "somehow warm." She became real even in death. The search that ended in the cemetery began a new awareness of himself as a more real person with a more complete history and sense of self. His identity was bolstered by the story of his birth mother's struggle to keep him and the story of his birth father's artistic career. Roger came to know himself more deeply and completely. In his own words, something inside relaxed, and he found himself able to move forward in his life with new energy and confidence. It was a resurrection of some sort for Roger. Even in death there can be new life.

The Hell of Not Being Known

The American Jesuit John Courtney Murray said about personal identity:

> Self-understanding is the necessary condition of a sense of self-identity and self-confidence. . . . the peril is great. The complete loss of one's identity is, with all propriety of theological definition, hell. In diminished forms it is insanity.[20]

Hell has often been described as being abandoned by God, the place where the Almighty does not know us, does not know the *who* that we are. This sense of not being known and the ensuing difficulty of not knowing ourselves may be precisely what the relinquished and adopted person deals with all along the way during the development of a self. As with all of us, adoptees need to know that they are known and need to know themselves deeply in order to discover the presence of God in their lives. If hell is the total loss of identity, then indeed heaven may be the place, even on earth, where we find our true selves, our real identities, even in a cemetery.

Chapter Four

Adoptee Intimacy: Heartache and Love

Intimate attachments to other human beings are the hub around which a person's life revolves, not only when he is an infant or a toddler or a school-child, but throughout adolescence and his years of maturity as well, and into old age. From these intimate attachments a person draws his strength and enjoyment of life and, through what he contributes, he gives strength and enjoyment to others.

—*John Bowlby*

Closeness is the way it is supposed to be for all of us who seek to live lives that are filled with the joy and enrichment that come with relationships. The connections that we make with others are the "love supply" that is necessary for our full development as human beings. This is especially true and especially critical in the first days and months and years of life. "Intimacy" is the word that we may use to describe this experience of being close to another, so close that boundaries melt away and union occurs in emotional and physical and spiritual oneness, whether young or old. But sustaining intimacy along the road of life is difficult because being close and staying close may constitute a threat of some kind, despite what may be the delicious wonder of love. For the relinquished and adopted person, who always lives with the twoness of the adoptive experience, the oneness of closeness can be especially difficult. For all of us, there are reasons to be wary of the trust that intimacy demands, but for adoptees, young or old, there are *additional* reasons to not trust the world in which they live and, instead, to fear the power of love. In the intimacies of human bonding, at whatever age or stage of development, there are possibilities of pain so deep that the self can be wounded or perhaps *rewounded* in a way that paralyzes, crippling the heartbeat of love.

At age ten Bobby walked into my office ready to sell me his story that nothing really hurt. He said that it did not bother him that he had been kicked out of summer camp for fighting nor did it hurt that he was ignored and rejected by other campers who had asked that he be removed because they feared having him around. It seemed that none of his fellow campers, or classmates at school, or the kids on the block where he lived liked Bobby. Neighborhood peers would steal his toys and break them. He had been adopted by religious, well-to-do parents who were conscientious in their care and their discipline of Bobby. Their spankings were getting harder because his behavior was getting more unmanageable. Who was going to win this battle for control of his behavior? From Bobby's perspective there was no great problem. He said that if others did not like him, he could handle that. He knew that he wanted his way and most of the time he was willing to fight for it, no matter what the consequences.

It *seemed* as if nothing was going to help Bobby, including me. Bobby worked hard not to let closeness happen with anyone. He was what might be called a very well-defended child. He reported that, when spanked by his father, he would not cry because he "did not want him to know that it hurt." Although the corporal punishments to which Bobby was becoming accustomed were within the boundaries of Colorado law (parental rights to spank), they nevertheless were, in fact, abusive; they pushed Bobby further away from all of us. Increasingly, it appeared that Bobby was defending himself against everyone, precluding his capacity for closeness with others and for future intimacy as an adult.

Then I took the lead.[1] I asked how he felt about being relinquished. Only then, in our fifth session of counseling, did this tough young boy become an honest tender boy. In several minutes, as our conversation about relinquishment went on, Bobby's eyes began to flow with the tears of sadness that he had so carefully protected himself from for so long. He pulled his T-shirt up over his face, wiping his eyes as he cried. There had never before been a place *in closeness with another human being* where Bobby could allow himself to be honest about his hurt within the adoptive experience. It was, for whatever reason, a subject clearly off limits at home (as for most adoptees), the very place where he needed to do his grieving. He said that he had never spoken the words that he told me that day. He "worried about his birth mother and wanted to know if she was OK." And then, as eloquently as he could, Bobby shared with me his truth: "I guess she didn't like me very much." No one liked Bobby very much. His whole world of people had become his birth mother. We had work to do.

Issues of intimacy in the adoptive experience span the entire life story of a person, *alongside* the issues of grieving and identity formation (already discussed) and fantasy (discussed in chapter 5). These four developmental issues coexist, as the adoptee grows toward adulthood, in ways that inform and impact each other, making adoptive development a unique developmental pathway. In this story Bobby's pervasive defense against his own pain about relinquishment, as well as his hurt from the spankings, produced a public persona. He appeared to be comfortable with whatever happened to him, but he precluded closeness to anyone. In his heart of hearts Bobby was alone.

Had Bobby kept this method of relationships in place, he might never have had the opportunity to dig deeper within himself. He might never have found out how much it hurt to be relinquished, or to think about being relinquished, or to deal with the blows of his current life. Nor would he have been sufficiently supported in terms of figuring out who he really was and who he wanted to be. Bobby, at age ten, seemed on his way to being tough on the outside and being very alone on the inside. In Winnicott's terms, his "true self" was carefully hidden from view and from review. Bobby's true self did indeed feel things, wish things, hope for things, and need things. That he was consciously aware of these emotions meant that the prognosis was positive. A more difficult personality structure might have kept his hurt well below awareness and out of reach of help and care.[2]

Nevertheless, this was the part of Bobby that could *not* be shared with his adoptive parents, especially when behavior that might be considered "out of line" by his parents meant the pain of a spanking. He was learning to hide from his parents the most important part of who he really was. Without intimate connection with his caregivers, these resources for further development, including the *capacity* to be close to others, were available only in a limited way.

Closeness is not only necessary for healthy, early development but also a developmental step forward as a person forms adolescent relationships and achieves the intimacies of marriage and family. For the adoptee, this occurs in concert with the grieving and the struggles with identity already discussed in chapters 2 and 3. This press toward intimacy is uniquely complicated at every stage of growth by the catch-22 of relinquishment and adoption. The connection to one's birth parents, as suppressed and repressed as it may be, may *of necessity* compromise how close adoptees allow themselves to be to their adoptive parents as well as to friends and then partners as development proceeds. A part of the self of the adoptee may remain unavailable for engagement in relationships because it has not been affirmed or integrated into the *who* that the adoptee really is. This dilemma may put the adoptee at risk in terms of building and sustaining intimacy. Instead of enjoying the connections between people, the adoptee may fear being discovered as the "bastard child" with all the shame and hurt that comes with the term. Or adoptees may fear being found out as somehow fraudulent, not fully real as persons, because there are indeed missing pieces to their stories. If the full disclosure of closeness is a threat, the relinquished and adopted person may understandably retreat from the assignment of learning how to become intimate with another human being. Although adoptees are not the only ones to struggle with closeness, they may be *more* concerned with its risks than their nonadopted peers. Their relinquishment sensitivity may preclude closeness in a tragic way.

Love has the power to heal much hurt. Bobby, for example, needed to know that he *was* lovable, despite his idea that his birth mother did not think so. But his behavior in relationships with people disallowed any corrective experience. *Relinquishment was a shadow that hung over his development as a boy.* The love, the deep caring, that he so needed could not quite happen. Bobby was at risk of never knowing what it is like to be truly known and accepted by another human being. A compromised capacity for closeness might have kept him stuck as an angry boy forever. But my honoring his connection and his struggle with his ghost parent story meant hope that things could turn out differently—that he could learn to love more deeply, and in the loving be healed of the sorrow that came as tears flowed down his ten-year-old cheeks.

Bowlby's Schema

During World War II many children were taken from the bombed-out streets of London and brought to the Hampstead Nurseries outside of the city. There they were cared for by people other than their parents, for reasons of safety or because their parents had been killed. The attachment behaviors of children from birth to age four were observed by Dorothy Burlingham and Anna Freud. A second series of observations of children in distress occurred at that time in several penal institutions. René Spitz and Katherine Wolf studied one hundred infants in the first twelve months of life who were cared for initially by their mothers and then "for unavoidable reasons" separated from them, not seeing their mothers at all, or at most once a week. John Bowlby drew on these reports, as well as others, to suggest that there was a "remarkably uniform" sequence of psychological processes on the part of these children in reaction to the loss of their mothers. Fathers, unfortunately, were not observed or discussed, much in keeping with the traditional roles of that day. Bowlby describes this sequence of *protest, despair, and detachment* as follows:

> [P]rotest lasts from a few hours to a week or more. During it the young child appears acutely distressed at having lost his mother and seeks to

recapture her by the full exercise of his limited resources. He will cry very loudly, shake his cot, throw himself about, and look eagerly toward any sight or sound which might prove to be his missing mother. All his behavior suggests strong expectation that she will return. Meanwhile he is apt to reject all alternative figures who offer to do things for him, though some children will cling desperately to a nurse.

During the phase of despair, which succeeds protest, the child's preoccupation with his missing mother is still evident though his behavior suggests increasing hopelessness. The active physical movements diminish or come to an end, and he may cry monotonously or intermittently. He is withdrawn and inactive, makes no demands on people in the environment, and appears to be in a state of deep mourning. This is a quiet stage, and sometimes, clearly erroneously, is presumed to indicate a diminution of distress.

Because the child shows more interest in his surroundings, the phase of detachment which sooner or later succeeds protest and despair is often welcomed as a sign of recovery. The child no longer rejects the nurses; he accepts their care and the food and toys they bring, and may even smile and be sociable. To some this seems satisfactory. When his mother visits, however, it can be seen that all is not well, for there is a striking absence of the behavior characteristic of the strong attachment at this age. So far from greeting his mother he may seem hardly to know her. . . . He seems to have lost all interest in her.[3]

Based upon these direct observations of infants in real-life situations, Bowlby offers a schema by which we can appreciate how the *child* may be experiencing the loss of a primary caregiver. The defenses that are set in motion are seen as understandable, given the pain of the parent loss. He presents a picture of hurt children dealing as best they can with the injury. Indeed, the separation and loss, the painful unavailability of parents, may have hurt so much that "psychological nerves get cut" in order to lessen the suffering and preserve basic functioning. But in so doing the child may be at risk in terms of ever having in-depth attachments in adult life. The deeply felt joy of living and loving may be less possible.

Bowlby describes what he calls "attachment behaviors" that he believes are instinctive and necessary for human survival. These are attention-getting behaviors initiated by the child instinctually for the purpose of receiving an adequate supply of both physical and psychological nourishment. In infants these behaviors include crying, smiling, following, clinging, sucking, and calling—behaviors that are critical for the bonding between a child and its caregiver in the first moments, days, and years of life. These are the behaviors that Bowlby observed and reported on in terms of time and intensity. When they were *not* successful in getting needed care, the problematic process of protest, despair, and detachment was set in motion. The result, as he describes it, is either an *anxious attachment* that is characterized by chronic worry about further loss, or varying degrees of *detachment* from superficial sociability to extreme withdrawal, depending on the depth of the pain. In either instance, something of great importance may be lost. Bowlby writes:

> There is a tendency to underestimate how intensely distressing and disabling loss usually is and for how long the distress and often the disablement commonly lasts. Conversely, there is a tendency to suppose that a normal healthy person can and should get over a bereavement not only rapidly but also completely.[4]

Relinquishment and Compromised Attachment

The question now to be addressed has to do with how well a fit can be made between Bowlby's observations of the distressed children of London so many years ago and the issues that confront the relinquished and adopted child today. There are some differences. His research would be most appropriate for considering the plight of the child who is relinquished and adopted at a young age. When there has been some time in which a child lived with its biological parents, the change in caregivers may be increasingly unmanageable as the years go by. Most "failed adoptions" because of an inability to make things work are of older children who cannot manage the change successfully. When relinquishment and adoption occur near the time of birth, there is not time for much emotional bonding to the birth parents or for real physical attachment to them, as was the case with the children of war. The earlier the wound of relinquishment occurs, the more open the question of the possibility and the capacity to connect.

The nature of the adoptee's loss, even at birth, is the open question. Like the nurses in the Hampstead Nursery, adoptive parents usually stand ready to care, offering the needed bonding and ongoing attachment necessary for development, in fact *more* than any nurse could offer. But the critical question that remains is how much the adoptee can *allow* in terms of care received. To whatever degree the adoptee protests and then despairs inwardly about the loss of birth parents, to that degree he may not be able to allow the very care that could be the foundation for the capacity to later love deeply. Bowlby points precisely to this dilemma, the catch-22 of adoptive development. When significant defenses are in place to manage the pain of parent loss, it may be difficult and frightening to let someone else in, even to help with the pain. And future relationships may of necessity lack the kind of intimacy that makes life full. If Bobby is to love deeply as an adult, he needs to allow himself to be loved deeply as a child.

Adoptee Romantic Radar

Why do we choose the people we choose when we "fall" in love? Why do we arrange our love lives in the manner that we do? Certainly all of us would like good, clear answers to this question, especially if our romantic relationships end up in painful conflicts, separations, or the agony of divorce. We sometimes wonder why the person we loved so much could bring so much suffering into our lives. It all started out so well when courtship began and gave birth to love in our hearts. How could someone so right end up being so wrong? This is a difficult but nevertheless important question to ask.

Why, for example, did Laleen marry three alcoholic men in a row, only to finally die from the effects of drinking at age fifty-four? What exactly was she trying to accomplish in those relationships? After all, her own father drank a good deal and treated her poorly. One would think that enough is enough and that she would learn to stay away from men who drink. Or consider the dilemma that a college co-ed talks about in terms of her attraction to young men. Two guys may be walking down a sidewalk on campus. They both look good in jeans. One is someone who would treat her well, buy her flowers, and be romantic and kind. The other looks away, has little interest in kindness, and treats women abusively . . . and *he* is the one that she likes. Why?

In what Freud describes as a *repetition compulsion*, we are often inclined to recreate our troubles of the past in the context of our present. According to this theory of human behavior, we inevitably find a way to play out the drama of our unresolved problems on the stage of our present life situation. We recapitulate our struggles of the past in order to repair the wound that still hurts. We do it again (and again) in order to master the difficulty, to resolve our suffering—to get beyond it. But the tragedy in this scenario is that real resolution of an intrapsychic difficulty may in fact be impossible with the person we have chosen. Sometimes people have to divorce in order to marry another successfully *if* in the context of the divorce they can work through their deeper difficulties. In an article entitled "Marriage: Crucible for Growth," pastoral counselor David Wurster puts this dilemma well:

> The unconscious directs people to choose partners who have the potential for bringing them face to face with some of their central life fears so that these fears can be worked through for further growth and mastery. In what Freud called the repetition compulsion people recreate in marriage their central life dilemma for themselves in order to work it through and this time to come out better. In this process only the person we really love and who touches our very roots has the capacity to drive us crazy as well as to help us find our deepest strengths.[5]

The idea here is that part of our motivation in forming our deepest relationships is that we (unconsciously) seek to recreate our troubles. We marry to make a mess, fix it, and come out the better for it. In such a frame of mind people can redo their personal dilemmas over and over and yet never learn the lesson that they are desperately trying to learn. The human heart is trying to mend, but sometimes cannot find a way to do so.

For our purposes, here is the question: *What if dealing with the pain of relinquishment becomes the organizing principle by which the adoptee arranges his relationships?* What if unresolved grieving about the losses of relinquishment and adoption stays hidden in a child's heart, unavailable to the healing that could come from being loved by another who knew and accepted the story? By this way of thinking, the issues of pain and loss in relinquishment may have much to do with whom the adoptee chooses as a romantic partner, the designated person whose purpose is indeed to assist in dealing with the ongoing hurt of relinquishment. There are many ways to play this out.

When Love Gets Stuck . . . Roadblocks to Intimacy

One option is simply not to develop relationships at all. If the need to protect one's true self from further hurt is all-pervasive, then the risk of relationships, in terms of the possibilities of being ignored or rejected, may seem too dangerous for the adoptee to consider. Of course, many reasons may come into play in terms of choosing to avoid people, not have friends, and not get involved romantically. Being alone may indeed be acceptable when the sense of security that comes with solitude is the chief objective. Human connections are sacrificed for the benefit of feeling safe, safe in a world that is perceived as potentially dangerous, that may take the adoptee back to pain that remains unthinkable. But aloneness is a high price to pay for safety.

A more common response or design for relationships is that of a *guarded closeness* with others, reminiscent of Bowlby's idea of *anxious attachment*. In this scenario, although closeness is compromised to some degree, a sense of safety is maintained in the midst of a relationship. Charlene, for example, was certain at first that she had married the right man. After all, there was never, in all twenty-two years of marriage, a day when Ed, her quiet, unassuming husband, asked for much in terms of real intimacy. Their sexual relationship was characterized by brief experiences of intercourse. Seldom were the emotional issues of the day put in words. Seldom were there times of personal sharing and support or times of disagreement or conflict. Nothing mattered much, and nothing much seemed wrong. As the years went by, their children came and went, growing up in a home where the rule was not to be too close. Only when moderate depression settled in did the deeper questions of Charlene's life come up for review.

When therapy began, the pastoral counselor, uninformed about relinquishment and adoption, did little to alleviate her symptoms. It was not until Charlene rediscovered a ring given to her in childhood that the process of counseling began to move forward. She recalled only vaguely her first years with a foster family that cared for her a good deal. When she moved to her adoptive parents at age three and a half, these foster parents had given her the ring. Her sturdy defenses against her sadness at last gave way to a flood of sorrow about the people whom she had lost. Her grief moved to search and reunion with her foster family and her birth parents in North Dakota. And Charlene "came alive" in ways that she had never lived before.

Now she wanted more from the marriage, and Ed was faced with the dilemma of responding in ways that she had never asked of him. Charlene realized that she had married him to be safe, to recreate her foster care, but now she wanted more. *The woman who married to avoid intimacy now wanted some.* She had been drawn to Ed to be secure. But the longing for a deeper connection to the people of her origins, her birth parents, erupted into new demands, changing the contract of the marriage. She now wanted Ed to do what he could not do, namely, be more close emotionally.

This resonated with the truth that she also wanted her birth mother, her ghost parent, to be close. Given the relinquishment and the secrecy around it, such closeness had never occurred. Charlene was tired of missing out, even though she had married to miss out. Now in the context of her relationship with Ed, this quiet distant man, she was redoing the drama of her relinquishment. After years of distance, of wishing to be close to the parents that in her mind had turned her away, she wanted more. Ed, her friend and lover, was now the enemy. Would he too decide that she was too much to deal with and, in Charlene's words, "get rid of me"? But Ed was not a candidate for closeness and never had been. In the drama of marriage came the trauma of relinquishment. It took many years, but finally things had become the mess that Charlene may have unconsciously intended all along. This way her heart could heal from the loss she experienced in the first days of her life.

In Charlene's story, the defense of guarded closeness gave way to the pressure of the need to recapitulate her story. Adoptees sometimes employ other defenses to guard themselves against the pain they don't want to face. One such method is the *need to control*. If everything is under lock and key, an adoptee may believe that he is safe, that he will never face the horror of being rejected again. The purpose of a relationship then is not simply to care and develop closeness as much as it is to guarantee, in bulletproof fashion, that the hurt that lingers in the heart will never happen again. In this scenario the adoptee's mate must defer and allow the control. Then things appear to be secure. The controlling adoptee has much at stake in terms of being careful to avoid the pain of relinquishment.

John was such a man. His marriage lasted six years. He was determined to run the relationship. He did this by telling his wife what to wear, where to go and not to go, what to do with her few moments of free time, and basically who to be so that he could always feel safe with things compulsively in good order. It was evident from the start that John was a frightened man whose use of control served to stave off his own anxiety. When he started to become almost paranoid about his wife's whereabouts, she moved to end the relationship, recreating the drama of relinquishment when she told him to move out. *That which he tried so hard to avoid came true in a desperate moment of truth between them.* Control only worked for a season. Much to his dismay, he had recreated his birth story for his own potential growth. But instead of growth, he opted for alcohol.

A more common type of relationship, in keeping with the role of the "good adoptee," is that of *being dependent*. This again is an attempt to guarantee security, in a different way. If you never cause a problem, if you always defer, if you do what others ask, if you always seek to please, then the reward should be that you are never rejected. But you live like a pet rock.

Leah was really good at this dependent role in her marriage. She worked diligently to please and to assure herself of a place in her husband's life forever. After several years of marriage, she came for counseling, wondering why she kept getting headaches on the weekends. It was puzzling because the stress of her life seemed to be in the middle of her week, working in human resources for a large company. Her story of adoption was a good one in that she recalls growing up in "a wonderful family" that afforded her lots of opportunities in life. But the issues around relinquishment were unexplored. Leah seemed so busy *being* a human resource to her husband and children that she had taken little time to care for herself or *be herself*, whatever that might have meant. As she began to hold her husband more accountable for his part of the relationship, his part of the chores of family life, her weekend headaches began to subside. Her anger began to make sense to her, and she discovered her strength in being so.

But the change went further, toward her realization that all her life she had been held captive to the fear of rejection. She played the role of the very good person, very good wife, and very good mother because of fear. She was not free to just be. Love at a deeper level, both from her husband and to herself, was always stopped by the risk of being discovered as somehow bad—relinquishable—and therefore Leah never took the risk of trying to be herself. Her headaches were the "friends" that she needed to lead her to freedom. As she and her husband renegotiated their marriage, new energy for living emerged, and Leah learned that, in her own words, she was a "keeper."

Sometimes adoptees are more direct. They never believe that they are lovable in the first place, and so they quickly put the connections they make in relationships in jeopardy. They may marry to *recreate the relinquishment* right away. Roger remembers with sadness the day, after three years of marriage, when his wife told him that "he had won." For three years she had tried to convince him that she loved him, but now she was giving up. She didn't think that it could be done. Enough of trying; she was out of it. As Roger recalls this sad story of loss, he remembers it *as if he said,* "Hello, I love you . . . you are going to reject me, aren't you?" So powerful can be the deeper forces that guide our behavior with others that we do *not* get the love and the care that each of us needs in order to be a whole person. But if we look again, we may see that those deeper forces are driving us to wrestle with our own personal demons, demanding that we take on the battle with the pain unacknowledged or unforgiven; take on the battle in the deepest places of our hearts where we do not forget, where our bodies and our souls remember the things that hurt, and where we keep the people who count. Relinquished and adopted persons are given the task of mending their own broken hearts in ways that at first may be difficult to discern. But when we listen to them carefully, they do tell us the story that they really want to tell, and of the pain that they really want to end.

When Love Goes Overboard . . . the Power of Connection

If love is the healing potion, then when we are in pain we may drink so deeply of it that it intoxicates us and we find ourselves overboard, no longer thinking wisely, but nonetheless deeply driven by the wishes that stir the heart. It should be no wonder that the relinquished and adopted person, as with many of us for other reasons, would at times drink deeply of the wonder that human connection in its many forms provides. After all, the hallmark of the adoptee's sometimes secret story is the wound of disconnection, of primal separation, from the givers of life. And, if this injury hurts so deeply as to alter one's life in terms of truly feeling loved, then the healing powers of creating love with another should be a wonderful alternative to the despair and loneliness of human isolation. No wonder then, that sometimes for adoptees love "goes overboard," that love flies like the wind and carries us to the heights of ecstasy, even if only in the fantasies that we attempt to hammer into reality. To believe that we are held dear by another, to be sure that we will be forever cared for and deeply appreciated, to know another in life and in heart, in skin and in bone, awakens in each of us the hope that our deepest pains will be healed and that our lives will finally be filled with joy. *The romance of persons is the return to the Garden of Eden, where in all our nakedness we are wondrously unashamed and free of all of the restraints of fear.* Adoptees know about estrangement and the wish for (re)connection in a way that none of us in the nonadopted population can ever fully appreciate. It is understandable, then, that sometimes for them, love goes overboard.

Adolescent Sexuality

With the onset of puberty, which is occurring now at earlier ages than ever before, the teenager faces the challenge of managing the overwhelming strength of libido. In all of our anxiety about sexuality as parents and as a culture, we continue to present our prohibitions of sexual behavior because, in part, we are fearful of the possibility of pregnancy for our daughters. This, of course, has special meaning to the adoptee, who knows full well that her birth parents did not hear the prohibition. In addition to the important identification with a birth mother, already discussed, comes the intensified human need for closeness, for connection with another warm, living human body, a closeness that may, if only for a moment, balance the hurt of primal disconnection. And so, quite understandably, the relinquished and adopted teen may discover in sex a healing possibility. After all, in the first years of life as an adoptee there may be a sense of discontinuity, a lack of matching in one's adoptive family, a quiet longing for a birth mother and a birth father who are both real and unreal, wished for but far away. Given these circumstances, sexual activity in adolescence, which we sometimes judgmentally label *promiscuity*, appears to be an attractive path. It is a powerful experience for such teenagers, which allows them to (re)connect to something inside themselves that they had lost. It also allows them to connect, if only for a moment, to another person, out there, a new person who carries the promise of replacing the persons who were lost in relinquishment. So love goes overboard. It ignites and sends the adolescent adoptee into a new world of possibilities of care.

Ellen's is such a story. With the divorce of her adoptive parents when she was fifteen, she faced a second round of losing parents as both her mother and father engaged in the conflict that often accompanies separation and divorce. She reported her feelings of abandonment, only vaguely aware of how this was a recurring theme in her development. She had been relinquished at birth and adopted at four weeks by parents who, for the first years of her life were attentive to both her and her older brother, also an adopted child. The report of her early years was unremarkable. She did well in school, was cooperative at home, and, in the words of her parents, was "just a great kid." However, with the onset of puberty—the beginning of the craziness of adolescence—Ellen began to pull away from her parents, as is normal in this stage of growth. Things seemed to be all right until one evening when she "just took off" with a boy she had met at a baseball game and had sex with him that same night. She reported her surprise at her behavior, wondering why it all happened as quickly as it did. She did recall that it was awkward because it was her first time, and that "it just felt good to be close to somebody."

Ellen became more curious about herself when this kind of sexual behavior started to be a pattern in her life. Over the course of a year, she slept with six boys and noticed that she seemed to be replacing them in her life rather than really grieving the losses of these relationships. Coming for counseling was difficult because she did not want to discuss these experiences or their meaning; she only allowed herself to wonder why she always needed to have a boyfriend when many of her peers did not. In some of the counseling conversations, Ellen was able to report cautious interest in learning more about her birth mother; Ellen assumed her birth mother was as sexually active as she was.

It appeared that Ellen's identification with her birth mother and her continuing interest in some kind of physical connection in her life were powerful forces, expressing themselves in a continuing story of sexual activity. It was so loaded with meaning for Ellen that it was difficult to manage. In rather typical adolescent fashion, she left the counseling process and continued to "act out" that which she could not quite see in herself: the understandable longing for real connection in a world that had given her only a short supply. Being relinquished and adopted; being the child of a difficult marriage that ended in divorce; being a girl-becoming-woman with all the excitement and fear that entailed—so much to manage in the early years of teenage life. No wonder that love went overboard in the life of this adoptee.

Genetic Sexual Attraction

Few of us imagine making love to our mothers or our fathers. For almost all of us in civilized cultures the idea of sexual relationships with family members never enters our minds. The taboo against incest is strong, and we don't let ourselves think about such behavior. But adoptees sometimes do. A telling, unusual, and little-known phenomenon that sometimes accompanies reunion with birth relatives is the explosion of unexpected sexual attraction toward a birth mother or a birth father, a birth son or a birth daughter, or sometimes a birth sibling. *The power of connection may become the power of erotic love.* In many stories of reunion between adoptees and birth parents the intensity of the connection takes on erotic strength and love "goes overboard" in a complicated, sexual direction.[6]

When Charlene traveled all the way to North Dakota to meet her birth mother for the first time, she was both excited and scared. The idea hit her that she was finally coming face to face with the woman whose body was her first home, whose heartbeat was the first that she had ever heard, whose *physical warmth* was the first she had ever experienced. Charlene recalls that she found herself staring at her birth mother. She remembers at times being embarrassed, caught in the stares that made this ghost parent real for the first time. But she could not take her eyes off her. The intensity of the wish to look and to touch surprised Charlene. Although she did not feel a specifically sexual interest, she was very aware of wanting to hold this ghost mother's hand, to feel the creases in her palm, to enjoy the warmth of nearness. *The dream of making up for lost time is a powerful myth as well as a reality in reunion.* For some adoptees, and for some birth parents, there is a strong desire to be together, look at albums of pictures, tell personal histories, span the years, and fill in empty pages with the missed seasons of the other's life. Sometimes this need to reconnect becomes sexualized, and the myth of "returning to the womb" feels like a possibility. In a profound and painful way those reunited can *not* make up for lost time. The wish to return to the primal scene of disconnection becomes all-powerful, and in the (re)connection of passionate love, adoptees and birth parents alike may think that they have a chance to resolve their lifelong hurt from the relinquishment. Separated birth relatives seldom think of this desire as incestuous, although it is. They sometimes think of it as a way back, a corrective, well-deserved experience of finally being with the person they have missed for so many years.

When Jenny called me from a city a thousand miles away, she was deeply distressed because she feared that she had forever lost her newly established connection to her birth son, Ray, who lived near my office. They had been in reunion for six months. At first their relationship had gone wonderfully well. Jenny had been invited into Ray's life in a way that was immensely pleasing. She had visited several times and met his wife and daughter. Now she was, for the first time, a mother and grandmother in real life. After her relinquishment of Ray, as is true with one-third of birth mothers, she had never married or had another child. It meant so much to now be part of her birth son's life. She recalls that, upon meeting Ray, her first impulse was to hug him, wanting to hold and hold and to never (again) let go of him. She also remembers her own puzzlement at finding him, her thirty-four-year-old son, very attractive. But in the "heat" of the moment of reunion she brushed this off as confusing. But the feeling, specifically the desire to kiss him, did not go away. She knew that she was sexually interested in her own son, as crazy as it sounded to her. It was both frightening and wonderful. She reports, "It made me feel so alive after feeling dead for so many years."

Ray would later recall that he had much the same experience. At their first meeting, he remembers being anxious and frightened that once more his birth mother might find him unacceptable and relinquish him again. When things went well in their first "hello," Ray became terrified because he found himself aroused, sexually interested in his own mother. How could he have such "crazy thoughts"? But his attraction to Jenny was strong, and he found himself pursuing the relationship and quietly living with the wish to be physical with her. For the first few months they e-mailed each other nearly every day. Both enjoyed the communication and each wanted to see the other again. From a distance it looked like a good reunion experience, which indeed is often the case. As the relinquished adoptee, Ray believed that he had "rediscovered himself" and was now "more complete as a person." That which was lost was found, and both were pleased with the changes that they experienced. They had found themselves in each other and they were happy, even excited, about living.

Until their most recent visit. Jenny's voice trembled as she recounted what happened. She had picked Ray up after work and they had gone to dinner, enjoying in-depth conversation about the years of their separation. They were both aware of the different levels of conversation: on one, they chatted with each other; on another, they longed for each other erotically. And then in the car they kissed, and the floodgates opened to passionate involvement that stopped just before intercourse. Each "confessed" that the long-distance telephone conversations had become stimulating, even for Ray to the point of having erections. Each wanted what was forbidden. Both Jenny and Ray were swept up in a tidal wave of romantic love that overwhelmed their sensibilities and smashed them onto the beach of incestuous connecting. Now Jenny was fearful that *once again* she had lost her son.

Her concern was well founded. Crossing the boundary and enjoying the Oedipal victory might have hurt them both. Obviously they had made a mistake. They did not use good judgment and, in the physical merger of mother and son, they risked their future together. Jenny was particularly concerned that Ray's wife would end the relationship forever, even if Ray did not. Their reunion was in great trouble. But why were they attracted to each other? Why did it happen in the first place?

The phenomenon Jenny and Ray experienced tells us much about the dynamics of adoptive development. This phenomenon, now called "genetic sexual attraction,"[7] also speaks to the meaning and power of human sexuality. It is "genetic," not in the sense that genes necessarily create these longings biologically, but in the sense that an adoptee, birth parent, or birth sibling may be attracted to a person of the same genetic bloodline. And it is certainly "sexual" in that these feelings of love are erotic experiences. But, again, why? *The answer has to do with sex and connection.* If the God-given purpose of human sexuality is not simply procreation, but also to further intimate human connection, then no wonder that the deep longings of adoptees for their ghost parents, or longings of the parents for their ghost children, become sexualized. The "drive" toward the other, both as object, meaning the lost other person, and as self-object, meaning the part of one's own self that is missing, may indeed become a sexual drive, a libidinal push toward another (discovered) human being. This person seemingly has the potential to magically erase the pain of relinquishment. Genetic sexual attraction is a powerful, primitive force that springs from the part of an adoptee's heart which may have been dormant for decades, but comes alive in the rush of love.

And in reunion, quite interestingly, this attraction is experienced as somehow right and normal. After all, by the rules set by adoption, incest would have to do with relations between the adoptee and his (nonbiological) parent or sibling, not with a strange person so long unknown. Put simply, relinquishment and adoption turn things upside down with regard to the usual "incest taboo." Love may develop in a puzzling way. That which is out of the ordinary, attaching to new nonrelated parents, supposedly becomes ordinary. Then another out-of-the-ordinary experience, sexual interest in biologically related parents or children or siblings, sometimes also becomes ordinary. And incest happens. The experience of relinquishment and adoption confuses the minds and the hearts of its children.

The configurations of genetic sexual attraction may be as varied as incestuous relationships in general. Mothers and sons, daughters and fathers, siblings and siblings, as well as same-sex relationships—all of these may play out in reunion. Four months after hearing a presentation on this subject to an adoptees' support and advocacy group, a woman wrote me anonymously about her reunion experience. She appreciated being "warned" about this unusual possibility. It was difficult for her to imagine that such a thing could happen. In her first meeting with her birth mother no such thing occurred. She wrote that she was relieved and thankful that she did not have to deal with this dilemma. After all, "who would want to think that you could make love to your own mother or father?" In conversation with her birth father (with whom also there was no sexual interest) she learned of the existence of a full birth sister who wanted to meet her. A month later she received a twelve-page letter and "a pile of pictures." She was surprised that someone else in the world looked so much like her. "My mouth dropped open, and I couldn't take my eyes off one picture for several minutes. Every detail of her arms, hands, and face were almost identical to mine. I was amazed." And then came the reunion, five months later.

> She arrived at my home and nothing short of death or disaster could have wiped the smile from my face. We got along from the first minute. Not only did we look alike, we walked alike, talked alike, moved alike, even laughed alike. But you see, I am a bisexual woman, and I can't tell you the number of times I have looked at her and wondered what it would be like to wrap myself up in her, hold her, kiss her. Believe me when I say that I would never think of following through with the images in my head. I value both her and myself too much, and I love her for the beautiful person she is. Moreover, I do not feel as though these thoughts are necessarily directed at her but more toward me. I look at her and picture it as if it would be making love to myself.

This adoptee has a beginning insight into the source of her sexual attraction to her birth sister as a self-object who could bring her forward toward a sense of being complete as a person. In part is this not what Eros is all about, finding ourselves affirmed in the arms and legs and heart of another? Her same-sex orientation served as her method of connection to others. In this case it made for the sexualization of her feelings toward her sister. Often adoptees and birth parents are surprised that in reunion, feelings of love for the other emerge from the deepest places inside themselves. These are the places where something precious has been guarded carefully and kept away from consciousness. Then in the moment of (re)connection all heaven breaks loose, experienced as sexual longing for the lost persons in their hearts, the lost pieces of themselves, and the lost dimensions of true love.

Is it any wonder that in the pretty brown eyes of a birth daughter a father would experience the rekindling of affection for the birth mother that he loved for at least a moment twenty-six years ago? Or that a birth daughter might see in the eyes of her father the dream-come-true of sitting in the lap of the father she never knew but often fantasized about, that he loved her?

Or can we understand the male adoptee who wants to be sexually united with his birth mother, who wants to return to the primitive, even prenatal warmth that he has wondered about and perhaps preconsciously remembered all his life? Can we appreciate the puzzled, frantic birth mother who never nursed her baby the two days before she unwillingly surrendered her infant to the closed adoption system, and never saw him again? She cried every year on his birthday and now, despite the years that have gone by, wants very much to take her grown son to her breasts and feel the warmth of his mouth. Is it possible to understand the plight of the adoptee who desires so much to be held by his birth father, to be close to the man that he wondered about for years, wondered whether this father ever cared, ever wanted to see him or know him or even question whether he, the son of his seed, was alive? Thinking about these questions can help all of us in the nonadopted world to appreciate the dilemma of the relinquished and adopted, the profound pain and ongoing confusion that comes with the exchange of parents, the inner grieving for the lost lover of one's soul, and the hesitant hope that reunion, deep (re)connection, can truly occur and restore life through love.

Incest is still incest, and sexual relationships such as these between reunited adoptees and their birth parents and siblings are always problematic and destructive. Crossing the physical boundaries between blood-related people, between mother and son as in the case of Jenny and Ray, always creates immense difficulties. The victory of Oedipus sleeping with his mother, Jocasta, proved to be his downfall in the great Greek tragedy. Acting on sexual wishes with ghost-parents-become-real is still incest and always proves tragic, creating more suffering in the lives of people already hurting. Accordingly, managing these feelings is critically important so that right in the midst of what can be the blessing of reunion tragedy does not occur. It is especially the responsibility of birth parents to be wise parents and set useful limits on sexual attraction, if it happens. They are still parents and need to be resources for their children.

For our purposes a useful interpretation of genetic sexual attraction is needed. In understanding it as a possible phenomenon of reunion, adoptees and birth parents can understand themselves more clearly if they feel such an attraction and find the inner resources to deal with it. In time, as reunited relationships begin to feel more normal (if normal is ever possible), such sexual feelings usually subside. Sometimes love goes overboard and takes us to places deep within ourselves where things unknown are discovered and where hearts are sometimes broken and broken hearts sometimes mended. It can take us to places where the ordinary wishes to be cared for become transformed into the extraordinary in the promise of sexual union, of deeply felt love. Adoptees go to those places too.

A Story of Love and Relinquishment

Ann recalls the mist of a cool summer evening when she walked through the trees, eager, expectant, hopeful that her life would change. Ann hoped that this would be the first of many conversations that might lead to love and a sense of permanence with someone else. At age thirty-two she had already suffered the agony of a painful divorce, fought out in court over precious little money and pots and pans. Two daughters and a son were victims of the war. It seemed that she and John fought the fight before the judge that they had never resolved in nine years of marriage. How could all the love with which they started, all the moments of passion that they had shared, end up in the name-calling feud that was still going on, two years later? He spoke to her little, refused to attend to finances, and seemingly sacrificed his children on the altar of divorce, leaving nearly all the parenting to her. Seldom did he visit his own children, despite all the stipulations of the final decree. He meant to punish her, even if his children never knew him.

As Ann walked through the pines, with their scent heavy in the evening air, she wondered if tonight might be the night when all her sorrow, collected over years of being ignored and abused, might change—change to the joy of being loved, of a kiss, of another's warm heart to be with and to be in. Two cans of Pepsi and off they went to their unknown, hoped-for future together.

Charlie seemed so different, the absolute opposite of her John. He was "incredibly sensitive," intuiting her deepest feelings. It was almost scary how he could know her feelings so well, so clearly when she was still "in a fog" about what she was experiencing. He listened, something she was not familiar with. Soon the two of them tumbled from the table of conversation to the grass with their first kiss. She knew that it was going to happen. And so did he, though he wrestled with the idea of making any commitment to Ann, something that he had had difficulty with all his life. But he kissed her nonetheless. Quickly the two fell deeply in love.

Ann had been relinquished at birth and adopted at two weeks by a couple well on their way to discouragement because of the pain and embarrassment of infertility. She was their bundle of hope, the only child they were ever to have. But adoption offers no solution to infertility or to the marital problems that her parents were having. Growing up was difficult in a home where Ann was so important to her mother but still never felt as if she quite fit. Her marriage to John had been a way out of trouble, only to find more. He, like her self-centered father, had for a second time put her through the pain of feeling optional, cast off from his view whenever she displeased him. So the end of her marriage was a relief, though she grieved for the hurt in the hearts of her children. In Charlie she hoped to find someone she could love and be loved by in a lasting, caring way. Their kisses were filled with the wonder of expectation. Making love was "like going to heaven."

But in truth he was never available to Ann in the way that she needed him to be. After three years of courtship, hours of conversation, and all the passion and care between them, he was still unsure. He said he wanted to make a commitment to her, but could not. Ann began to see that that was true, and in a moment of heart-breaking pain she announced that the relationship was over. "It is over because it has to be!" she told him with tears flooding her swollen eyes and running down her cheeks.

At a variety of levels reality had, once again, made its harsh way into her life. Once again she felt relinquished. Not important enough for the sacrifice of "freedom" that Charlie could have made. Once again she felt optional. For a *fourth* time she felt the sting of rejection in her heart, in the place where the deepest issues of her life were carefully kept. Her birth parents didn't care enough to keep her, so she thought. Her adoptive parents had tried to solve their issues in her life so unsuccessfully. John had had his way all too long at her expense. And now this. But with the words "It is over because it has to be!" Ann announced her freedom from the past, from being unimportant.

In the deep grieving of the loss of her love, again she experienced the pain of long ago. But she also relinquished something. She achieved the unfortunate but necessary developmental task of letting go of the need to wrestle with her rejecting ghost parents, to recreate her pain. The words about being over because "it has to be" *also* fit the relationship between an adoptee and a birth parent because relinquishment is real. Making believe that relinquishment, especially by her birth father, who refused to see her, could somehow be ignored or undone had kept Ann's love life in continuous chaos.

Ending the relationship with Charlie was a painful moment in her life. Ann had gained control over a part of herself that had always kept her unimportant. Now Charlie, like her ambivalent birth father who was unable to commit, was out of her life. She could let both of them go. Now she was free to live within the boundaries of reality without redoing the past. Releasing Charlie, as good as he sounded, was cutting loose the need *to find someone to whom she could be unimportant.* She marched away from him, with sorrow felt deep down, in order to try again, more wisely, with someone with whom there could be a future.

Letting go of being let go may at times be especially difficult. It may hurt to the core of one's being. *If the pain of relinquishment remains as the guiding principle by which one determines one's life, then love and life never quite work.* Only when the patterns of romantic experience are identified can adoptees see themselves differently, grieve their griefs, reconstruct their identities, and form lasting, intimate relationships—relationships that are free of the sorrow that comes with lost love. But it is not an easy thing to do. Often there is pain in the story.

Chapter Five

Ghost Parent Wonderings: The Challenge of Fantasy Resolution

You know, it was like I saw her, and it was like, there goes everything out the window. There went the fantasies, the wanting to know, everything was a big relief. I mean it was like, it's over. I don't have to wonder anymore.

—*Krista, an adoptee, telling of her reunion with her birth mother*

We as human beings do not let go of each other easily. Our relational strength, our ability to be image-bearers of a relational God, can be ultimate and intense. If connection to a person has been deep, and we lose this "loved one," we may hold on tenaciously, using any parts of our life together that we can find, any poignant memories, or special mementos, songs, pictures, or places that give meaning. Part of our humanity is demonstrated by our capacity to grieve deeply, with one hand wiping our tears and the other holding on tightly to the person who has meant so much, who has touched us deeply, and who has given us life in a variety of ways.

Well, what about losing someone who has literally given us life itself? When Marlou Russell, an adoptee and psychotherapist from Santa Monica, California, met her birth mother for the first time, she wrote:

She was nothing like I had imagined. When I was a child I was sure she was a movie star hopelessly in love with her leading man but unable to be with him for some obscure but romantic reasons. When I was a teenager I thought she was probably a drug addict living on the streets. Why else had she not come back to claim me or at least inquire about my well-being? Meeting her goes into that category of significant and life-changing events that I will never forget. . . . I was adopted as an infant in what is called a closed or traditional adoption. I was not supposed to meet my birthmother. She was supposed to forget me and get on with her life. We were supposed to ignore the fact that something out of the ordinary had taken place. Losing the mother who gave you life is traumatic. I wanted to keep a part of her in my soul, and I thought about her a lot. My fantasy life about my birthmother was rich, since I didn't have a lot of facts to counteract what I imagined. I wanted to believe that if my birthmother and I were in the same place at the same time we would immediately know it and recognize each other. For years I peered at faces in the crowds—was she here? I was always looking—at the grocery store, in movie lines, and later, even in bars. I wondered if she ever thought of me. Did she remember my birthday? I had lots of questions that I wanted to ask her. I wanted to see her. I wondered if I looked like her. I wondered if I looked like anyone.[1]

It should be no surprise that adoptees almost always report that they wonder about their birth parents, that they fantasized about them both as children and as adults, and that sometimes they seek reunion with them when law and circumstance allow. They refuse to "forget them" and live life without them. Even relinquished infants may strive to keep connection with the lost ghost parents.

A rich fantasy life is *often* part of the adoptee's experience, especially as a child. Not knowing about birth parents (who they are, where they are, how they are), and not knowing about why they chose to relinquish their child— all these things stir the imagination of the young adoptee. Many adoptees report that they remember daydreaming, musing, and wondering about their birth parents all along the way of development. Sometimes they simply imagined. They made believe that these ghost parents were kings and queens far away or that they were just greasy-spoon waitresses or wayward men. All the time they were wondering (but they seldom asked anyone about it). The world of make-believe, of fantasy, is a place where many relinquished and adopted people, especially inside the closed adoption system, have lived to some degree.

Although we are speaking of play, of fantasy, it is not an insignificant matter. Living in the undefined world between fantasy and reality may pose problems for the adoptee. First of all, getting a grip on reality may be more difficult for adoptees than for those not relinquished and adopted because adoptees are without all the parts of their stories in place. Second, having the delightful freedom as a child to make believe about other, better parents is interrupted for adoptees by the reality of actually having other parents, the ghost parents. And third, perhaps most importantly, maintaining some form of connection to these ghost parents becomes a very important, albeit difficult and conflicted, developmental task for the adoptee. This chapter will show how the exchange of these birth parent fantasies for images in reality, to whatever degree possible, constitutes a fourth developmental challenge for the adoptee, alongside grieving, identity formation, and managing intimacy.

The world of make-believe is a wonderful and important place for children. It is the world of play, of toying with ideas and thoughts and images, of putting them into play in a way that helps the child make sense out of her realities. Birth parent fantasies are here taken to mean the content of daydreaming, wondering, musing, thinking, or imagining about these ghost parents in whatever form these may be presented by the adoptee. These fantasies come in many shapes, sizes, and colors. For the relinquished person, they may be secret nuggets of gold that are treasured because of their great connective value.

Some personality theorists assign an important role to childhood fantasy life, suggesting that, even in later life, it may be critical to adult functioning. Psychologist Eric Klinger, for example, observes the following about daydreaming:

> Our minds constantly flit from one thought to another and one type of daydream to another. . . . Psychologists usually label thoughts as daydreams if they are about something apart from the person's immediate situation, are spontaneous and are fanciful (with things happening that are contrary to reality). I view daydreams broadly . . . as reactions to what is happening outside or inside us; fantasies about the ordinary, everyday things as well as extravagant flights of fancy.[2]

Klinger's study of daydreaming suggests that daydreams serve the positive purpose of easing boredom, with two-thirds of daydreams "focusing on the person's immediate situations and tasks, and the rest dwelling on other tasks, past and future, and relationships."[3]

This last category is the interest of this chapter, and it fits well with Klinger's observation that "emotion and current concerns are intertwined with one another and with our daydreams."[4] He notes that although for many years daydreaming in children has been held in disrepute, "associated with laziness and even craziness,"[5] it is now considered a *positive* resource for creativity and problem solving.

Imagination is the mental process we employ to create a fantasy, be it of birth parents or whatever. It is the way by which we give birth to a new idea about something or someone not (or not yet) real. By way of imagination we "come up with" ideas, thoughts, and fantasies. Research psychiatrists Linda Mayes and Donald Cohen describe imagination as a mental apparatus that "begins in the earliest symbiotic interactions between mother and infant"[6] and continues to take shape as the child develops and moves on to relationships with others. They see imagination as

> the process of creating mental images in the service of wish fulfillment or defense [which is] evident in the products of dreams, symptoms, children's play, parapraxes [slips of the tongue, etc.] and tranferential phenomena.[7]

Imagination, which includes the creation of fantasies, is viewed as an important part of psychological development. It allows the child to deal with relationships with people who are not present. *Creating a mental image of a parent who is not available fulfills the wish to be with that person and also defends against the pain of the loss of that person's presence.* A fantasy of a birth parent may be the synthesis of memories and percepts of that person which keeps the adoptee psychically alive, thereby avoiding the pain of abandonment.

Mayes and Cohen put it this way:

> [T]he *need* for an imaginative capacity comes into being as the child wants or desires those individuals whom he does not or cannot have at that moment. The fantasies of the . . . child express, and in some ways gratify, these desires. . . . Evoking a mental image of the other is part of the ability to know that the other is absent and to look for that person.[8]

Such a fantasy becomes part of the inner subjective world of the child. Such fantasy making can be thought of as "becoming unrealistic in the service of reality."[9] It serves the adaptive function of allowing the child-becoming-adult to test reality in a variety of frameworks, "trying on" different images of people in order to develop in-depth attachments to them. In this way, fantasy serves as a pathway toward a deeper appreciation of reality. It becomes a way of testing reality by way of contrast and approximation, which leads to adult perceptions of what is real. For adoptees, who may be fantasizing about the where and the what and the why of their birth parents, fantasy affords them the opportunity both to maintain connection and to defend against the threat of the fear and hurt of loss as they put together their own real stories as relinquished persons.

A Good Grip on Reality

"What is REAL?" asked the Rabbit one day, when they were lying side by side near the nursery fender, before Nana came to tidy the room. "Does it mean having things that buzz inside you and a stick-out handle?"

"Real is not how you are made," said the Skin Horse. "It's a thing that happens to you. When a child loves you for a long, long time, not just to play with but REALLY loves you, then you become Real."

"Does it hurt?" asked the Rabbit.

"Sometimes," said the Skin Horse, for he was always truthful. "When you are real you don't mind being hurt."

"Does it happen all at once, like being wound up," he asked, "or bit by bit?"

"It doesn't happen all at once," said the Skin Horse. "You become. It takes a long time. That's why it doesn't often happen to people who break easily, or have sharp edges, or who have to be carefully kept. Generally, by the time you are Real, most of your hair has been loved off, and your eyes drop out and you get loose in the joints and very shabby. But these things don't matter at all, because once you are Real you can't be ugly, except to people who don't understand."[10]

The Velveteen Rabbit asks the same question asked by adoptees: "What is real?" Many times they report that they don't feel "quite real" as they live their lives from day to day.[11] Somehow something is missing which denies them a full sense of authenticity, of being *fully* in reality, as if parts of themselves are unknown and caught up in mystery. If, as the Rabbit suggests, becoming real is a matter of being loved until your "hair falls off," it may well be that adoptees who have parts of themselves unloved, unacknowledged, unmirrored may indeed have understandable difficulty experiencing life as human beings feeling fully real.

The dance between the reality of pieces of the self that are well-known and the mystery of other pieces that are unknown may be especially difficult if the relinquished and adopted child has learned early on *not* to wonder, *not* to be curious, and *not* to think about his birth parents. Unfortunately, this has often been the case. Adoptees have been put in a difficult bind in terms of needing to know their stories and learning to feel guilty if they ask. When adoptive parents have been unable to resolve issues around the loss of their own biological generativity (having their children by birth), they may feel uncomfortable dealing with the realities of unknown birth parents who are reminders of infertility. They may make believe as well, imagining that their adopted children are indeed not relinquished by others and not needing to know and to grieve. Unfortunately, this leaves adoptees without the freedom to explore the reality of their relinquishments. And so the world of fantasy may become the only safe place for an adoptee to be with his story.

Adoptees and the Family Romance Fantasy

One of the interesting contributions that Sigmund Freud made to the body of psychoanalytic theory is his presentation of the dynamic that underlies the "family romance fantasy" he and others observed in latency-age children. This fantasy is that of having *another* family, having other parents who are caring and always wonderful . . . in marked contrast to the "wretched experience" of living with the present parents, who respond inadequately to the needs of the child. The fantasy often leads children to express the wish to be "returned" to these other parents. The child believes that, once returned to these people who somehow lost the child, she would be treated well by these (idealized) parents and thus returned to the (royal) status that she deserves.[12] According to Freud, the function of such a fantasy is to ameliorate guilt and anxiety about incestuous and hostile wishes toward the parents, allowing for separation from them, and thus resolving the (normal) ambivalence that a child may have toward the parents. This helps to achieve a new level of independence from them. The "romance" of another family then serves a useful developmental purpose. *But what about the adoptee, for whom there is* in fact *another set of parents, out there somewhere, who did indeed lose the child?* What is the impact of this reality on the adoptee's ability to fantasize, specifically as this relates to the other family romance?

Researcher Herbert Weider suggests that the impact is negative. His study, based on his own in-depth work with three adoptees, suggests that "knowing one is adopted results in modifications of the [romance] fantasy and that certain types of adoptees seem incapable of effectively creating the paradigmatic family romance fantasy."[13] Weider points out that usually children react with alarm when they learn that some children are relinquished and adopted.[14] The reality of relinquishment and adoption changes the fanciful pleasure and developmental purpose of imagining royal care from another set of (true) parents into the stern realization and possible fright that children are indeed taken away from their parents. Accordingly, in Weider's view, the adoptee is at a disadvantage because the freedom to create new (wonderful) parents with their corresponding usefulness in the world of make-believe is curtailed. The (other) parents are not simply in imagination—they are in the realm of reality. They are real but "ghost" parents, a reality that is confusing.

These are the ghost parents with whom the adoptee must someday deal and address in his own subjective world. Paul Brinich describes this phenomenon as the "double representational world"[15] of the adoptee, which complicates normal development. This phenomenon sets the stage for a split-life experience, living a life of two selves, one with each set of parents.

Weider reminds his readers that for every child, "[n]ecessary to the fantasy form and function is an imagined good and loving parent who never disappoints the child nor arouses sexual longings."[16] With relinquishment and adoption, this fantasy component, as a wish and as a defense against Oedipal involvement, is not in place. The reality of missing birth parents breaks in and interrupts the imagination. Now the adopted child is left to wonder about the reality of relinquishment. In contrast to the normal other-family romance, the child may need to return to an idealization of his adoptive parents as a line of defense against the (devalued) birth parents who "gave me away." In Weider's view the results are clear:

> Knowledge of being adopted led to excessive dependence on the adoptive mother, an accented belief in the probability of the fantasy's actualization, devalued images of abandoning biological parents, and phobic avoidance of references to adoption.[17]

The adoptee, without the opportunity for romance about another family because of the reality of relinquishment, is left wondering about bad, hurtful parents instead of wondering about good, adoring parents. This, for a child, is no small difficulty to overcome. Further, the adoptee is left with *fewer* resources in fantasy to construct parental representations that may be useful in the development of a healthy, well-esteemed ego, which could sort out and accept the more difficult dimensions of reality. Put simply, the world of imagination may be *less* available to adoptees as a resource for growth. Reality gets in the way, and imagination turns in new directions.

Winnicott and the Infant-Caregiver Bond

Despite the ancient myth of Romulus and Remus, who were allegedly reared by wolves, Donald Woods Winnicott, perhaps the best known of the object-relations theorists,[18] makes it clear that the founders of Rome could not have made it without "the ordinary devotion of a human mother."[19] Children cannot grow up without parents. With proper food and clothing they can develop physically, but without the presence of a parent they cannot mature as persons who are emotionally adult or spiritually well. The major emphasis of Winnicott's writings is the primacy of the mother-infant relationship as the central building block for the healthy development of children. His writings reflect careful attention to the critical importance of what happens at the beginnings of life, the very vulnerable time when most relinquishments occur.

> I am putting forth . . . that, at full term, there is already a human being in the womb, one that is capable of having experiences and of accumulating body memories and even of organizing defensive measures to deal with traumata (such as the interruption of continuity of being by reaction to impingements from the environment in so far as it fails to adapt).[20]

With regard to the first days of life when, with relinquishment and adoption, an exchange of parents may occur, Winnicott raises his concerns:

By the end of two weeks any baby has had plenty of things happen that are entirely personal. At the age at which an adoption becomes relatively easy to arrange each baby has been so stamped with actual experience that the adopting parents have a problem of management that is essentially different from that which they would have had if the infant had been their own and in their own care from the start.[21]

Winnicott does not apologize for his bias that a child's birth mother is usually the best person for the nurture and the care of that child. Although he is quick to acknowledge the value and necessity of adoption (war-torn London, besieged by daily bombings, left hundreds of infants and children without parents), he insists on an appreciation of the possible complications that may occur with the relinquishment and the adoption of a child. Of the process of adoption he writes:

> [W]hen you plant a child on parents it is not just a question of a nice lit-tle distraction for them. You are altering their whole lives. If all goes well, they will spend the next twenty-five years solving the puzzle you have set them. Of course, if things do not go well, and very often they must go badly, then you are involving them in the difficult task of disappointment and the toleration of failure.[22]

Winnicott emphasized the importance of early placement, teaching that adoption should take place as early as possible in the life of the child.[23] In his view, no matter when adoption occurs, there is always a *muddling* of things when the relation between the mother and the infant is interrupted. Such a break in "the continuity of being," as in the case of relinquishment, always has a cost. Simply put, according to Winnicott, attachments to adop-tive parents can never "reach to *the most primitive levels of their [the adoptees'] capacity for relationship.*"[24]

The need to construct birth parent fantasies may relate directly to this psychic and spiritual fee for relinquishment and adoption. The substitution of parents puts an infant or a child at risk because even if a child is adopted at birth—in the delivery room—there is still a "changing of the guard," a replacement in the child's original environment. The question that each relinquished child must address has to do with how to survive this great interruption.

Fantasies as Transitional Objects

As an infant begins her psychic journey from the world of merger and magic, where simply thinking causes things (like breasts) to be, to the world of shared reality, where things (like people) exist in their own right, inde-pendent of the child, there is, according to Winnicott, a process of bridge building in what he calls *intermediate space*,[25] where there is not yet clarity between what is *me* and what is *not me*. It is in this fuzzy, difficult-to-define area of very early experience that Winnicott makes an important contribution by his description of transitional objects.

At age three and a half our youngest son walked across the alley behind our home with his "blanky," a torn, dirty corner of a blanket that he had sucked entwined with thumb for over three years, and handed it *without grief* to our neighbor, telling her, "Give this to the baby, I'm a big boy now." His blanket was a transitional object, used to negotiate the transition between knowing that his mother and I were there and *believing* that we were there.

Transitional objects are the things (usually soft things) that children employ to build a bridge between the merged boundariless world of the infant-mother relationship, "where fantasy and reality are one,"[26] where the infant can create his world because its mother is present, and the world of object relations, where the "insults" of reality are accepted and the child understands that mother may or may not be present. Winnicott describes the transitional object, the first "not-me" possession of a child, as residing in a place in the child's experience which is neither entirely subjective, as a reference to an internal object, nor entirely objective, as a reference to an external object. These are precious things in a never-land, a wonderland, which is neither real nor unreal. In Winnicott's own words, "the question is not to be formulated"[27] as to whether blankets or teddy bears are things that come from within or without. They are the inhabitants of an intermediate space between the world of grand illusion and the world of harsh reality.

In this world of intermediate space, according to Winnicott, important emotional development is occurring as the infant-becoming-child attempts to hold onto the experience of omnipotence (in merger with the mother), all the while facing (in micro steps) the reality that relating is a *shared* experience with others who are others. He writes:

> I am here staking a claim for an intermediate state between a baby's inability and his growing ability to recognize and accept reality. I am therefore studying the substance of *illusion*, that which is allowed to the infant, and which in adult life is inherent in art and religion, and yet becomes a hallmark of madness when an adult puts too powerful a claim on the credulity of others, forcing them to acknowledge a sharing of illusion that is not their own.[28]

It is within this world of illusory experience that transitional objects play an important role in terms of maintaining a child's emotional health as well as offering adults moving cultural and spiritual experience.

Birth parent fantasies may be just such an experience for the person who is re-

linquished and adopted. Although Marlou was thirty-five years old when she met her birth mother, it may well be that for all those years she was "keeping her alive" in the world of fantasy, of make-believe ideas about her birth mother, as either a movie star or a drug addict, in order to maintain her own well-being and keep a *connection* with her ghost parent mother. Psychologists Alan Sugarman and Lee S. Jaffe make such a case for fantasies being a more advanced form of teddy bear–type transitional objects because of the manner in which they may function to maintain connection to parental images.[29] A fantasy may serve to "hold" in reality someone absent or unavailable for nurture. Our son's "blanky" helped him hold his mother (and, I hope, me, his father, too) close to his heart until he learned to trust that we would be there. Then, without grieving, he let go of the blanket.

In the magical land of transitional space, birth parent fantasies may function as transitional objects do, guaranteeing an ongoing relationship to the ghost parents of the adoptee. No sealing of adoption records or changing of birth certificates can erase the reality of their existence. They may stay alive, even for a lifetime, in the form of fantasy so that the primal connection between an infant and its first caregiver can be maintained. Just as a blanket or a teddy bear restores a crying child, so the fantasy of a birth mother's care can soothe and calm and reinforce the belief that the ghost parent is present, even though she is absent. The birth parent fantasy is thought of—touched, we might say—whenever it is needed. When the absence of the birth mother is experienced and the connection is (temporarily) lost, the fantasy, as a transitional object, comes to mind to reassure the child. And, just as the child will hang on dearly to his "blanky" when feeling frightened, so the relinquished and adopted child may hang on dearly to his birth parent fantasy when comprehending and thereby experiencing the pain of abandonment. Thus, it may be that only in fantasy, even as many years go by, can many adoptees in a closed adoption system keep connection to longed-for-birth parents.

Birth parent fantasies may also be thought of as unusual forms of transitional objects for at least three reasons. Transitional objects, first of all, receive their psychic life from the continuing, steady, reliable presence of the objects/persons they represent. Again, in Winnicott's familiar words, the child's task is to "be alone in the presence of someone." He writes: "The basis for the capacity to be alone is a paradox; it is the experience of being alone while someone else is present."[30] Developing this "capacity to be alone" hinges on the very presence of the "good enough" mother/caregiver. And, as this person continues to be reliable and present to the child, the child slowly learns to trust, to take in the meaning of the transitional object and then slowly to relinquish the object without mourning. Because its meaning has been taken in, it is no longer necessary, and it is discarded without grieving.

But for the birth parent fantasies, thought of as transitional objects, this process does *not* unfold because the object represented is *not* available for continuing nurture. The birth parent is gone. This object absence means that the relinquished adoptee is left *without* assistance toward psychological development out of this intermediate space toward new psychic land where fantasy and reality are more clearly distinguishable. Instead, birth parent fantasies may become the objects of fixation, frozen in time, in which the adoptee gets stuck. The transitional object assumes a different, reified status. It is "alive" but running in place, helping the adoptee to simply survive in a strange place. Without the nurture and the continuing, steady, reliable presence of the birth parent, the relinquished and adopted child may simply hold onto birth parent fantasies well into adult life in order to keep the relationship alive, avoiding psychic death, *if only in fantasy*. No wonder that adult adoptees sometimes report that they do not feel fully real. Part of them isn't, at least not yet, at least not until the hidden part of themselves is validated, as it may be, in reunion with a birth parent. Their birth parent wonderings become endless wanderings in their minds, going to no new place because the light of reality is shut away from their eyes.

A second reason that birth parent fantasies are unusual forms of transitional objects is that they may take very negative forms. In contrast to the warmth of a soft "blanky," the image of a lost mother is a very different experience for a child to manage. A devalued, negative image of a birth mother sets up pain as much as security. Internalizing the truth may mean dealing with the negative, even shameful truths that often surround relinquishment. There is less joy about assurance of care from a loving parent, if only in fantasy, and more gnawing pain that dawns with the awareness that one was "given away." The negative content of some birth parent fantasies makes them a mixed experience, so that sometimes they may be stopped consciously and repressed into unconscious regions, the hidden places, of the adoptee's mind.

Third, birth parent fantasies, as unusual forms of transitional objects, may most often be characterized as struggles with ambivalence. Carrying *mixed* images of birth parents is rather common for adoptees. As they grow up, they develop the ability to move beyond rigid positive or negative views of these ghost parents and proceed to form images with less splitting into good and bad ideas, and more wondering about both the strengths and the weaknesses of their biological parents. It is an exercise in ambivalence, imagining both good and bad about birth parents. It is a mark of maturing to be able to do this as opposed to designating birth parents as only good *or* bad, without integrating pluses and minuses into one picture. It is, nevertheless, a difficult picture to keep in one's mind, and it is markedly different from simply enjoying an idealized view of a parent. This experience of ambivalence with birth parent fantasies that remain unresolved into reality may account in part for the ambivalence that adoptees feel about themselves as relinquished and adopted persons, people with "mixed" origins.

To summarize, from a Winnicottian perspective, birth parent fantasies may be thought of as both usual and unusual forms of transitional objects, which, regardless of their content, serve the important function of connection to lost love objects. In the wonderland of the adoptee's intersubjective space there may be, *still living*, still stuck in illusory experience, images of care and of consternation which keep one's developmental story going, keep it moving toward a future moment when fantasy may be exchanged for reality and more peace may come to a troubled heart.

The Adoptees in Search (AIS) Study

In 1993, I interviewed seventeen adopted adults concerning their birth parent fantasies, as part of a dissertation study.[31] These subjects were members of an adoption support and advocacy group in Denver called Adoptees in Search. Each was in the process of searching for his or her birth parents. Lengths of searches varied from three months to twelve years. Ages ranged from nineteen to forty-nine. Four subjects were male; thirteen female. All subjects were Anglo-American people.[32] Each was asked to relate the content and the possible utility of any fantasies that they currently had or recalled as children. It is, first of all, interesting to note that *all* seventeen subjects reported that they did indeed have such fantasies. It is also important to note that *none* of these people had ever been asked about this "secret" side of their life stories. Nor had any volunteered this information to another. The interviews were new experiences of self-disclosure. Evidently, their birth parent fantasies had been "off limits" for discussion and review, by themselves, by their adoptive parents, and by others.

Content of the Fantasies

The material that these relinquished and adopted people presented comes together as a collage of disjointed images, of faces painted in both bright and dark colors, with both approving smiles and rejecting frowns, some close up and some far away, some fragmentary and some full-blown images of both wondrous angels and evil monsters. They are the creations of children at play, the important play of making sense out of relinquished and adopted experience. Whether as children, as teenagers, or as adults the authors of these fantasies sometimes go into vivid detail to capture their experience of wondering and keeping alive the images of their own life givers.

The content was predominantly concerned with life status (thirteen of seventeen).

> Well, I thought that they would be rich. . . . I really had bad thoughts. I imagined her being a waitress in a greasy spoon diner-type of place. . . . I imagined her as being someone who was, you know, not making much money, not doing very well. I pretty much kept the same fantasy . . . she's still a waitress at a greasy spoon.

These searching adoptees put the life experience of their imagined birth parents under the review of what "they might amount to," judging them by societal standards of success. The balance between positive and negative views of these ghost parents was relatively even.

Fantasies sometimes alternated back and forth between positive and negative views of birth parents (nine of thirteen women).

> I pretty much kept the same fantasy. Always thinking in the back of my mind, well, maybe she's rich, maybe she has a lot of money. Maybe there's, maybe she's done well in life, you know, but pretty much in the front of my mind, No, she's probably still a waitress in a greasy spoon.

For some there was a pattern of moving from one kind of fantasy, recalled in childhood, to another that emerged as growth and development continued. This change in fantasy formation went in both directions, from negative to positive (five) and positive to negative (four). (Adults with more negative views often reported more hesitancy about searching because of a greater fear that the outcome would be negative.) One subject remembers a recurring positive fantasy that changed to despair:

> Well, first I thought that they'd . . . I'd find them and they would be rich and they'd take me away from these people and this and that. They're going to come and take me away and give me a life that I wanted. That kind of thing. Then, as I got older it went, it started, like when I got into high school, I was thinking, well, they must be dead on the street somewhere or else they would have found me by now.

Another remembers change in the other direction as life went on:

> I used to make a comment about, Oh, my mother was probably a hooker and my dad was probably in a ghetto . . . a bum in southern Nebraska. . . . And then I kind of went from that to the fact, I think it was more as I started getting closer to doing this [searching], then my thoughts were . . . you know, I've ran into a couple of businesses in my business that were in Nebraska and I kind of joked, Oh yeah, my mom's probably the president of the company or something. And I think I went from this horrid fantasy to now hoping that she's like Miss Wonderful, you know . . .

Male adoptees reported no ambivalence or change with regard to birth parent fantasies (four of four men). Whereas many of the women in this study reported mixed feelings and changes in their fantasies as the years went by, the men reported images that did not change through the years. Two had no fantasies about birth fathers at all. The other two saw them in a negative light. "He'd probably be embarrassed to meet me," and "He wouldn't care." Images of birth mothers were mixed. "She probably tried to find me" was balanced by another man's view, "She's probably weak, not strong-willed. She won't stand up for herself, she won't stick up for her family." Another reported an image of his birth mother in glowing terms:

> I've got a caricature of her. I imagine her with blond hair, flowing. A sense of peace and calm and a vibrant, a vibrancy too, and I view her face. And it's angelic or it glows like that of a woman you just made love to. . . . I see, I just, I see eyes and blue and a nice Raphael-like in terms of image. Idealized.

Rescue fantasies were a common theme (six of seventeen).

> We had a summer cabin up north and I always fantasized about being able to stay there (at the cabin) by myself and live in Wisconsin because I, for some reason, felt that was where this person, this perfect person, was going to drive down the street and take me away.

Adoptees who remembered a positive fantasy of a birth parent in childhood would often include, as part of the ascribed goodness of the parent, the belief that the parent wished to retrieve the subject as a child and the belief that it would someday happen. One recalls:

> I imagined her coming up to Mom and Dad's house, coming to the front door and telling my parents that she wanted me back. I remember fantasizing that she would come to the door. She'd changed her mind and she wanted me back.

The idea of rescue, of deliverance from the loss and distance created by relinquishment, seemed to be an important part of the fantasy life of these searching adults.

Birth mothers were much more in focus than birth fathers (sixteen of seventeen). In the course of the interviews, questions that concerned *birth parents* were often answered in reference to *birth mothers*. Unless specific questions about birth fathers were asked, they were not specifically mentioned. So much have birth fathers lurked in the background of the stories of relinquishment that even searching adoptees tended to forget about them. Comments like the following illustrate the point:

I never thought about him. He had never entered my mind. It was just, Mom had told me, "Your mother gave you up," so in my mind my mother gave me up. She never said that your mother and father could not care for you, it was just your mother. So I never thought about my father, never.

It was like he wasn't there. It was like there was no such thing. I never thought of my father, I mean I would say this pretty much is that I don't think I would have even thought about my father in that process, even if I could remember fantasies about my birth mother as a child. I don't think my father would have been there.

Material presented with regard to birth fathers was brief, less-developed fantasy. Birth fathers were most often seen in a negative light, as disinterested parties to conception and birth, who had little to offer the searching adoptee in terms of care.

I figure if we track him down I will be very bold about it and go up to him and say, "you . . . bastard whatever, whatever, whatever. I won't give him a chance to reject me. I'll probably reject him first.

Well, I imagine him in a business suit. Probably, he went on and had kids of his own. . . . Of course his kids are probably grown by now, but I don't imagine that he really ever thought back about what he did.

The birth father played a different role in the fantasy life of searching adoptees, as a passing thought in history (and possibly repressed for future thought), whereas the focus on birth mothers was central to the fantasies and stories of the subjects in this study.

Adoptees remember stopping their fantasies (seven of seventeen). One of the more interesting discoveries in these interviews, unexpected and unsolicited, was the report by one-third of the subjects that they could recall very consciously making a decision to stop their daydreaming, their wondering about their birth parents. It was as if, for them, they could only tolerate so much of it and then, for whatever reason, they would decide to stop it. One woman reported such an effort in detail:

I wanted to know what she was like. I mean, I tried not to, my mom always told me 'don't' . . . but just the impression that I got was I wouldn't fantasize about her, I didn't know if it was okay or not. I just didn't want to because when I knew someday I would meet her and I wouldn't want my expectations to be demolished or something. . . . I remember I just stopped. It was like, that's stupid, just forget it. I don't know if I thought other people would think it was weird because I couldn't talk to anybody about it. . . . I didn't want to talk to my mom and I didn't know what to do, so I just stopped it.

A decision not to fantasize was part of the mix for several of the adoptees, who could only go so far with their imaginations and would then need to stop, turning their heads and their hearts away from wondering.

These interviews were often emotional, cathartic experiences (ten of seventeen). Embedded between the lines of transcripts were many tears. The subjects of this study were very eager to tell their stories and also troubled in terms of doing so. Answering questions about birth parent fantasies often opened the door to deeper levels of awareness of pain and hurt surrounding relinquishment. The conversations were triggers for more grieving within the process of the interview itself. People reached for tissues as they talked about their childhood wonderings, about struggles with a sense of self and impoverished self-esteem that centered around being given up, the primal wound of the story. Here is one illustration of the hurt:

> After I decided to search, the fantasies went absolutely wild. I'd have nightmares that who I found was an evil person and that why I had been relinquished was that I was evil too and I'd find that out about myself, that I was truly an evil person. So I deserved all the terrible things that could ever happen to me in my life because I was such an evil person and I did not deserve to be loved [tears].

The depth of emotion in many of the interviews contributed to the richness of the material. As some adoptees told their stories of relinquishment and adoption, they found themselves in a great deal of pain. Some expressed appreciation for the opportunity to be heard and understood. Their tears and their sighs gave credence to the idea that what is going on in the fantasy lives of adoptees, young and old, is emotionally charged, important experience.

The Question of Utility

When adoptees were asked what role they thought that their birth parent fantasies played in their lives, they experienced the question as unusual and sometimes mystifying. Reflecting on their fantasy experiences is very different from simply reporting them. Comments made while describing fantasies were sometimes just as revealing as answers to the questions asked about the role of their fantasies. Most of the adoptees had little to say beyond the first comment that came to mind. They enjoyed telling their experience; they struggled to interpret it. Nonetheless, clues to the usefulness of birth parent fantasies were offered in these conversations.

Several ideas emerged which were helpful in terms of understanding how searching adoptees saw the role their birth parent fantasies played. Some were concepts around which comments clustered. Others stood alone as useful insights into the "why" of a given fantasy. Both positive and negative fantasies served a variety of purposes for these adoptees, some of which they were only partially aware. These clues sometimes overlap and often leave as many questions as they answer. But together they serve as a beginning toward understanding what may be going on in the mind of the adoptee.

Connection (eight of seventeen). This is an important word to adoptees. Very much in keeping with a Winnicottian appreciation of fantasies as transitional objects, the idea of connection, albeit conflicted connection, was prevalent in the comments about the role of fantasies. One woman talked about the fact that her birth mother fantasies "gave me something to look forward to" in terms of her wish, specifically, for reunion and the reconnection that such a reunion would bring. Her comment is typical of many who could not articulate details about the need for connection, but hinted at it as an important reason for the existence of a given birth parent fantasy.

> I suppose it served a purpose of keeping me continually thinking that I need to find an answer, maybe I guess, you won't get the answer until you locate your birth mother. I don't know that it helped me or hindered me, that's just the way it was.

> My fantasies connect me. That takes off the shame I've put on myself in the rejection. Back to them, back to their scenarios. And it gives me myself.

Identification (thirteen of seventeen). The search of the adopted adult is a search for someone else in the world with similar looks, with similar personality traits, with similar values. One woman states it this way:

> I would spend hours looking at myself and it just didn't make any sense to me. It was like, how could I be Italian [as she was told], and I always used to lie and say I'm Irish. On Saint Patrick's Day I'd want to go, 'Yeah, I'm Irish,' because I couldn't figure out, like, how could I possibly be Italian and have all these features. So that screwed me up even more about envisioning, like, who I was supposed to be.

Another reports:

> I don't know how a mother can give up her child and not be hurt by it because she carried me for nine months. We were connected, we were part of each other. And I think I do have some sense of who she is. Whether or not, how clear it is or focused right now I don't know. I just wonder what commonalities there might be. Yeah, I am curious.

The search includes discovering missing pieces of the self, and, often, adoptees would describe how curiosity and fantasy about a birth parent could possibly fill these voids of identity. Even fantasied identification with a birth parent might help to fill the empty places in the adoptee's self-image.

Validation and affirmation (five of seventeen). Birth parent fantasies helped some adoptees to see themselves in a better light. Some used the fantasy, cast in positive terms about a distant ghost parent, to bring home a positive self-image, a proclamation of the goodness of the adoptee, especially for a child growing up in difficult circumstances. Positive birth parent fantasies were useful to some relinquished and adopted persons because they were a hedge against low self-esteem and self-devaluation. Someone out there, the ghost parent, affirmed them as persons, made them feel good about themselves, if only in fantasy.

> The fantasy based on the nugget, the little sliver of information I have is that, Hey, I'm okay. . . . It was validation. I mean clearly we are fellow travelers. What I am doing is not so weird. . . . It's absolute affirmation! I think I want both of my parents to be gorgeous-looking people because of my low self-esteem.

Protection from pain (six of seventeen).

> Q. What role did it play for you to be able to think about your birth mother?

> A. Kind of an escape. I probably would have gone insane if I hadn't done that.

These words are from a woman who struggled as a child with adoptive parents who refused to allow her to even discuss the subject of adoption. She also reported rescue fantasies throughout her childhood, hoping consciously to be delivered from what she described as emotionally abusive parents. For her, the birth parent fantasy helped her to deal with pain *at home.*

For most other adoptees in the study birth parent fantasies sometimes took a negative form in order to protect them from the pain from parents *out there*, the pain of the rejection of relinquishment.

> I imagined her being a waitress in a greasy spoon diner-type place and maybe that was just to protect myself from thinking that I would be better off living with her, being raised by her. I think as a protection for myself I just imagined her as being someone who was, you know, not making much money, not doing very well.

For other adoptees positive rescue fantasies served to "take the edge off the rejection" by keeping hope alive that the primal wound of relinquishment was a temporary difficulty. One woman said:

Countless times I can remember sitting in my bedroom, especially after I had been punished or sent to my room for something, looking out across the lawn at my secret place and thinking maybe if I go over and sit there somebody will come down the street, this perfect friend will come down the street and take me with them and my life will be perfect from now on.

This fantasy stayed the pain of relinquishment by keeping her from facing the permanence of the loss of her birth parents while she was growing up, shielding her from what might have been a pain too awful to know.

The expression of anger (four of seventeen). Birth parent fantasies were sometimes seen as convenient ways to clarify and express the anger that comes along with the rejection which in some ways is always part of relinquishment.

I figure if we track him down [hunting language] I will be very bold about it and go up to him and say, 'You . . . bastard whatever, whatever, whatever.' I won't give him a chance to reject me. I will probably reject him first.

The final decision was me saying, "No. I don't want you, I want my parents.' Even at that age, I don't know how and I don't know why, but I always thought, you know, hey, you don't want me, why did you mess around in the first place, you know. I was very angry, very hurt, and I took that hurt out on my [adoptive] parents.

In these fantasies the anger at the "primal wound" of relinquishment took the form of an imagined confrontation with birth parents in which the adoptees did the rejecting and evened the score. Anger also appeared to sometimes be an underlying issue in the construction of negative, devaluing fantasies of birth parents.

Separation from adoptive parents (three of seventeen). One insightful adoptee made this comment about breaking loose from a sense of obligation to her adoptive mother:

Well, it helped me break the relationship with my adoptive mother. Obviously, I can't if this is not only a woman who decided to raise me or I wouldn't have been in this home. That they closed in, gosh knows when, and the strong message was, 'You wouldn't have lived here if it wasn't for me. I rescued you and you're obligated.'

In describing her birth mother fantasy this woman also spoke of "hoping to meet a friend. To not be a secret [person], to be somebody [a birth parent] that she can openly love." This idea was useful as a hedge against her demanding adoptive mother. The fantasy allowed her to separate herself from a sense of obligation and control. It served in her mind to help her emancipate herself.

Freedom and acceptance (three of seventeen).

I think it was all about, like, Oh my God, what if that's what I find? How am I going to handle that? And then there's part of me that says, 'Oh my God, you can handle this because you . . . thought that your whole life, you know. So, and it kind of set me free, like the very first time I thought, I told another human being that I was conceived, that my thing was that I believed that I was conceived by white trash and that's that, that was what it was all about for me. My mother was poor, a waitress, no support for herself, and didn't want to be stigmatized with having a child out of wedlock.

This adoptee's words, "it kind of set me free," are a reference to another role that such fantasies may play in terms of releasing relinquished and adopted people to become adults who are able to accept the reality of their origins. Her report of the ability to tell others, "Well, that's that" may represent the beginning of her freedom to be herself as a relinquished adoptee. The truth had to some degree set her free.

In summary, relinquished adoptees, who were seldom able to bring their ideas about birth parents out into the light of day in conversation with their parents and friends, may have made significant use of fantasy as a way to explore their ongoing relationships with these ghost parents. They used these fantasies to maintain connection with them, even though at times this meant also employing them to manage serious pain about the loss. Throughout childhood and into adulthood, many fantasies "stayed" in the recesses of the minds of adoptees so that, at very deep levels where these people so often hurt, there was a secret place where adoptees could go to work on their ghost parent struggles.

Reality as the Better Option

Even bad news is good news because it is real news. For a variety of reasons our Anglo-American society has sought to keep a good deal of the truth away from the minds and hearts of adoptees, even those who are adults. "Protecting" adoptees from the truth about themselves has had negative consequences that no one at the time (when adoption records were closed) predicted, but which nevertheless need to be examined today because of what we now know about adoptive development. Keeping ghost parents as ghosts has meant denying adoptees the sense of being fully real as persons. Something has always been missing, whether the adoptee thinks about it, senses it, or *not*.[33] Unless the whole story is told, no matter how painful the story may be, the adoptee does not know or have his whole story. In an effort to search for and find his birth mother, one adoptee named Jerry found himself on the steps of a state hospital in Colorado where he learned that she was a paranoid schizophrenic. She suffered from a thought disorder so significant that she had no memory of the story of his beginning. It was a great and deeply felt hurt to meet her after nearly thirty years of not knowing. But the meeting brought the richness of truth, even pain-filled truth. Jerry met his birth mother in the hospital and he met himself in completing his story. Simply put, not knowing one's birth parents or birth story or medical history leaves many relinquished adoptees with a sense of unfinished business with life. This in turn may hamper the development of the adoptee as a person, a complete person, with a clear sense of identity, and sense of peace about the story, even if it is a painful story.

Efforts at search and reunion were once thought to be the mark of poor connection between an adopted child and her adoptive parents: if the relationship was healthy and strong, why would the adoptee need to find the biological parents? *The truth may well be the opposite of that belief. Adoptees who have the blessing and encouragement of adoptive parents to learn their whole story and who meet and relate to their birth parents, in appropriate ways as they grow up, may have the best chance of a fuller and more meaningful life.* A life with secrets is a life with strings to a buried history that anchors part of the person in the darkness of shame, embarrassment, and ignominy. The light of truth sets us free; it is truth that adoptees must know if they are to be fully free.

Resolving fantasy into reality, even painful reality, is a developmental challenge for adoptees that may be incredibly difficult. They may wonder if the truth *is* too awful to know. Winnicott calls it the "unthinkable anxiety"[34] of the loss of a parent/caregiver. Nevertheless, adoptees are challenged to do the additional intrapsychic and interpersonal investigation if they are to put *all* the pieces of the puzzle together as adults. There is simply no alternative to the truth about oneself that will mitigate the diminishing forces of secrecy and shame. For this reason search and reunion activity needs to be understood as a useful tool in the adoptee's continuing self-construction. We can no longer believe that keeping birth parents within the darkness of locked adoption files, under the shadows of hidden history, or behind the closed eyelids of fearful children-becoming-adults will not exact a price in terms of the fullness of living. As has often been said, "Reality is the best defense."

Closing Comment

Portraits of ancestors set in the atria of Roman homes or carried along in the processions of family funerals served as the idea from which the Latin noun *imago* and the verb *imaginari* derive.[35] It is by way of imagination, by fantasy, that many adoptees keep alive images of birth parents and ancestors in the atria of their minds. In the daydreaming and wondering of everyday life, relinquished and adopted people keep their connections with their ancestral history and hold these images "alive," even as they grieve the "death" of the ghost parents whom they never knew as parents. They may hold dearly to their mental portraits of these loved ones for many years. Such is the power of connection in the human heart.

Chapter Six

Keeping Hope Alive:
Despairing about Relinquishment

*I've often prayed . . . if I never see her on this earth . . . if only
someday, I would see her in heaven.*

—*An adoptee, reflecting on reunion*

Hope, because it is hope, is always elusive. The human experience for many
is that of holding on, as best we can, to hope—hope that our futures will be
good. But held, as it is, in Pandora's box, hope is very much a possession of
the gods. We seek hope from the human side of things, but divine forces
are very much at work. As the Greek myth goes, Pandora was driven by curiosity (as are many adoptees) and opened the box, despite the instructions
of the conniving, angry Zeus. Then, once the lid was opened, all forms of
biting, stinging, evil creatures flew out to plague humankind forever. Zeus's
vengeance against Prometheus was accomplished and Earth was cursed.
But one creature remained in Pandora's box—hope.[1]

The Greeks considered hope to be an evil curse, an illusion, something
else to irritate humans. In their minds, the future was sealed and inevitably
delivered by Fate. Hope, accordingly, was considered a useless irritation,
the "food of exiles" (Aeschylus), and "man's curse" (Euripides).[2] According
to the Greeks, hope served no good purpose: it was an unfortunate and unnecessary dabbling with the future. The future was already determined, so
why hope? It was good that it remained in Pandora's box, kept as a possession of the ancient gods of Greece. Hope has always been a possession of
the Divine that men and women seek after and wrestle with, not as the biting snare of Greek mythology, but as the foundation of religious faith.

Hope is often the spiritual force that drives the lives of adoptees. Relinquished and adopted living is an experience that may include hoping for lots of things. Hoping at age ten that a birth mother is OK, or hoping that a birth father would show up at the front door and "take me away," or hoping that losing birth parents "will not hurt when I grow up," or hoping that maybe someday the kids at school will quit saying that "your mother didn't love you!" Hoping as a teenager that you can figure out who you are even if you do not know your birth story, or hoping that you can meet somebody who looks like you, or hoping that getting close or intimate will not create too much fear about being rejected. And, then, the big hope—hoping that there will be a day when you can meet your birth parents, both of them, and touch them and see them and feel them and know them as friends in your life who care about you—no matter what happened years ago. So much of being relinquished and adopted is about hoping . . . even to the point of being careful *not* to be too hopeful.

Hope as a religious concept is presented in this chapter as a theological construct[3] that helps us to define and explain the spiritual experience of adoptees as people who hope. By the word "spiritual" I mean the dimensions of human experience in which a person relates to the greater forces of the universe, which most of us call God. This spiritual dimension of life involves the perception of oneself as a creature limited by time and space in the face of larger powers and processes that are beyond our control. By the word "theological" I mean the manner in which we think about and understand God. This involves our understandings about how God is involved in the world and in our lives. And by the term "religious faith" I mean the belief system with which people interpret and comprehend their experiences of God.

Hope Defined and Contrasted

In the book of Romans the apostle Paul writes that "hope that is seen is not hope, for what a man seeth, why doth he yet hope for?" (8:24). The very essence of hope has to do with looking toward the future, which is not yet realized, a vision "not yet manifest." Once hope is fulfilled, it becomes something else, a positive experience of a new reality, but it is no longer hope. For many adoptees the ghost parent struggle is a struggle with the reality and the meaning of birth parents "not yet seen." They are quietly hopeful, longing not only for the faces of these people but also for the positive meaning that such a meeting, "whether on earth or in heaven," might offer. The ghost parent struggle is a struggle with hope.

To hope is to take a positive stance toward the future—to long for something better, something that heals and restores, makes present difficulties more tolerable, and gives present effort meaning because of future possibilities. As a theological construct hope is the belief that there is indeed a benevolent presence in the universe, God in some form, that will act for a person's benefit in the long run of life. Adoptees dare to hope that their lives can go well, despite a tough start. They are people who hope that the "primal wound" of relinquishment will not be the organizing principle of their lives, but instead, that good experiences of care and understanding will offset the difficulties of being relinquished. They are hopeful that the future will heal the past.

Hope does not need to be there when things are fine. Gabriel Marcel writes that "there can, strictly speaking, be no hope except when the temptation to despair exists."[4] It is only when the chips are down, only when life is painful, unfulfilled, or meaningless, that hope comes to play as a light on the trail toward the future which motivates and energizes. Psychologist Paul Pruyser, a student of the study of religion, writes that hoping only really occurs when one

> feels trapped, is visited by a calamity, or has come to the end of one's rope in understanding or deed. . . . Hoping presupposes a tragic situation; it is a response to felt tragedy, and it is the positive outgrowth of a tragic sense of life. . . . In order to hope one must first have some sense of captivity, of being caught by the limitations and sorrow of the human condition, in firsthand experience.[5]

Hope is not the muscle of willing nor the bravado of optimism nor the defensiveness of denial. Willing, the "power of positive thinking," is volitional, having to do with a cognitive act. When one is willing something, the ego is very much in charge. Willing is an important and useful component in making one's life successful. However, it fails to touch the deeper question of one's relationship to God. Optimism certainly seems similar to hope. But there is a difference here as well. It has to do with the distance with which one deals with life. Optimism implies a positive outlook, but it does not reach for the places in the human heart where an awareness of God is part of the story. (It is a good attitude, but it is not tied into the goodness of God.) And hope is also distinct from denial because genuine hope does not avoid any aspect of reality (as adoptees are often tempted to do), but embraces that reality and seeks to address it with all the resources that can be marshaled.

Therefore, hope is characterized by a unique spiritual responsiveness[6] to the struggles of life, including the ghost parent struggles. Hope is *believing*, being certain that, despite the hurt that today has brought, tomorrow will be different, that "tomorrow waits with joy." There is a certain humility in hope because the goodness of God is really the issue at stake. Hoping is trusting that the future will unfold in a useful way, not because of all our efforts, but because in some ultimate sense God is caring.

Holding on to such belief may be difficult when nothing seems to work, when as many as twelve years go by without a "break" in getting information that could lead to a reunion. Daring to be hopeful may be exceedingly difficult when the hoping itself brings up the pain of the losses. In the lives of some relinquished and adopted people, staying hopeful has its limits, and at times there may only be a thin thread of hope, only a glimmer of a good future. Adoptees may live between hope and despair as they face questions without answers and grieve without pictures. Honestly facing the challenges of adoptive development may mean dealing with the temptation to give up hope, to despair, to lose belief in a loving God. The "temptation to despair" exists.

The Centrality of Hope

It may well be that hope is the most important foundation for an adoptee who is navigating the challenges of growing up. Hope, as a theological construct, is so central as the foundation of religious faith that James L. Muyskens, in his book *The Sufficiency of Hope*, argues that "religious commitment be placed in the realm of hope rather than that of belief."[7] Building on the work of existential philosophers such as Immanuel Kant and John Stuart Mill and existential theologians Søren Kierkegaard and Gabriel Marcel, Muyskens develops his perspective that hope is the most adequate basis for faith. The evidence for belief in God, theism in its many forms, comes up short in terms of any convincing, logical argument. But hope, he suggests, is a better foundation for religious faith because it more honestly captures the experience of people as creatures who hold out for the future, for the works of God in human life.

"The question of God's existence," Muyskens writes, "is the question of the possibility of an open future."[8] And this question most centrally has to do with hope. Hope gives human experience the beginnings of a transcendent dimension. Hope keeps us aware of possibilities yet to be experienced, aware of longings that sometimes transcend present reality, and it keeps alive a vision of a better day. Certainly, this is the experience of relinquished and adopted people who secretly keep alive a vision of a day to come when questions of relinquishment are answered and pictures of birth parents come alive in flesh and bone. Hope for the whole story, hope for a different feeling about self, hope for closeness, hope for completeness—these are the "not yet seen" treasures of many adoptees. To the degree that God is a benevolent caring God, to this degree adoptees put their faith in hope that this is so, and that the future will prove it to be so. Hope becomes central to the adoptee endeavor.

The Grounds for Hope

It is one thing to hope, as daring as that might be; it is another to have some reason, some grounds for hoping. The parent, for example, who hopes to visit with a child though the child has died, is "hoping against hope" in a way that refuses to recognize reality. A person in a psychotic state might hope unrealistically that the world would stop turning on its axis. This is also groundless hoping. Yet these examples raise the complex question of how far one might stretch in hoping or, conversely, how thin one's grounds might be for hope before one stops hoping. Inside the closed adoption system, the hope of many adoptees at times seems very thin, especially when all possible resources for search and reunion appear exhausted. It is in this in-between place, between hope and despair, that faith is born, comes to play, and becomes the reason to hope anyway.

We can think in various ways about the grounds for the foundation upon which hope is built and depends. Traditional Christian theology, which has its own struggle with how hopeful it dares to be, given the fallenness of humankind, has grounded its hope in the single historical event of the resurrection of Jesus Christ. This viewpoint suggests that hope for all humankind hinges on the reality of that moment when death was overcome and Jesus, the Christ, walked forward from the grave into a transformed life. A positive view of the future is based on the positive outcome of the Easter event. Emil Brunner, a traditionalist proponent of this perspective, asserts:

> It was by Christianity that mankind (sic) was taught to hope, that is, to look to the future for the realization of the true meaning of life. The peoples of Asia, the peoples of the pre-Christian world never looked to the future with hope, that is, with the expectation that it would bring realization of the true meaning of life. These religions are all ahistorical or nonhistorical in a double sense: they are not *based on a historical fact or revelation* as is Christianity, and they do not look forward to a goal of history as the full realization of its meaning.[9]

From this point of view, hope for the future, despite Brunner's skepticism about "progress,"[10] is grounded on and depends on the historical and personal reality of Christ's resurrection; only in the light of this "fact" can the future be seen positively as the final fulfillment of the promises of Christ, including eternal life and a new heaven and a new earth.

Adoptees well appreciate the importance of historical events. Their relinquishments and their adoptions were profoundly important historical moments. Although it is relatively easy to see how an adoptee would "bank" on the moment of adoption as grounds for a future hope, it is more difficult to see how the moment of relinquishment could be grounds for being hopeful. And, as noted before, unless the relinquishment is managed in a successful way, it may not be possible to take full advantage of the hope that adoption offers. Being rejected at birth, no matter what kind words are used to describe that relinquishment, is hardly grounds for hope at first view. But what if the birth parents were ambivalent about that decision? What if they did *not* want to release their child? What if, as was often the case in Anglo-America fifty years ago, the birth mother was forced to surrender her baby to adoption, despite her own protest, spoken or unspoken. It is difficult to protest when you are a teen mother, pressured by parents and society to relinquish. Is it possible that such fragments of relinquishment history are grounds for hope? Adoptees may know pieces of their story from their adoptive parents, or they may create them in fantasy in order to "have" them anyway. Hope that is genuine dies hard. Adoptees may be hopeful in the face of all the hurt of relinquishment because they are able to hang on to bits of knowledge and the belief, against all odds, that they mattered at the time of relinquishment.

Within Christian theology the proponents of a "theology of hope" (Braaten, Moltmann, Pannenburg) propose another emphasis as the ground for hope, namely the future itself. They suggest that theology is really driven by eschatology (the study of the future). The future pulls the present forward in an open-ended fashion toward something that is good. Carl Braaten, in *The Future of God*, writes:

> The starting point of Christian theology is not at the beginning but at the end. What Ernst Bloch, the Marxist philosopher, puts forth as an ontological assertion we therefore adopt as our theological slogan: "The real genesis is not at the beginning but at the end." Eschatology, not archeology or protology, is the source of life and light. The past and the present are illuminated by the light that dawns in the morning of God's future. The Christian faith originally began from the power of God's creative eschaton. His eschatological word became flesh; revelation became history; the end of God's way with man was attained in a preliminary way through Jesus' resurrection unto new life; the last judgment of God is proleptically actualized even now through his justification of the godless by sheer grace. The eschatological orientation of Christian existence looks to the future as the decisive mode of time. The categories of hope and futurity are at the core of Christian faith.[11]

Braaten believes that Christian theology must reposition itself; not looking backward to one (albeit important) moment in time, but forward to the future as the continuing revelation of God's presence in our lives. He argues, therefore, for the "primacy of hope in human existence."[12]

Jürgen Moltmann, in an essay entitled "Religion, Revolution, and the Future," continues this theme, grounding hope in an emphasis of the future goodness of God. He argues that "faith in God has been saturated more with anxiety about the future than with hope in a new future on Earth."[13] Instead, Moltmann argues, the anxieties of our existence, "the terrors of our time,"[14] need to be met by a new confidence in the future, characterized by hopefulness. He writes:

> Today in all dimensions of life we are searching for a future in which we can really hope. For only such a future can inspire our present work, give meaning to our present sufferings, and intensify our present joy. More radically than earlier generations we know that we live in history where everything changes and nothing remains in its place. We live "between the times."[15]

Moltmann is critical of traditional Christian faith with its search for "paradise lost," its longings for its origins. From his perspective, this view is uninformed by eschatology, constantly defeating itself and leaving no openness to the future. He argues for a "new interpretation of reality" that takes its beginning point in the future, grounding hope in "the all embracing vision of God . . . which imbues concrete hope with an urgent and ultimate character"[16] in still unrealized future experience.

The adoptee can relate. Although searching for origins is especially significant for adoptees, often not much is known about the past that feels hopeful. Though bits and pieces of relinquishment history can carry some signs of hopefulness, the past may carry even more pain and more reasons for despair. Looking to the future, as theologians of hope suggest, and seeing possibilities for different scenarios of care and connection may be very useful for adoptees. The "future stories"[17] of adoptees, first imagined and then pursued as life goals, can bring hope in a way that looking at the past never allows. Imagining a letter from a birth mother, hearing a word about one's ghost parents, envisioning a reunion in the middle of an airport— these future possibilities can indeed give meaning to present experience, if only to have created something to anticipate. The longing for people from the past, transformed into excitement about the future, can make "present sufferings" more manageable. Believing that the future can be better can be grounds for being hopeful—other adoptees make it, others figure it out, others find their birth parents, others do it . . . so can I! If God is a caring God, God can make such things happen. Adoptees may need to depend on unrealized futures to make present experience tolerable in ways that few of us in the nonadopted world ever understand.

One of the most influential theologians dealing with the nature of hope is the French Christian existentialist Gabriel Marcel. He grounds hope in neither a past moment of history nor in a still unrealized future, but in human experience itself, specifically in *transcendent experience*. His contribution to a theology of hope is entitled *Homo Viator* (Man the traveler), which he subtitles "Introduction to the Metaphysics of Hope."[18] He begins his discussion of hope by way of reference to the conditions of existence that make hope both necessary and possible, namely the state of "being a captive or a prisoner."[19] In this situation, which he suggests is characteristic of much of human experience, a person is invariably constrained from "rising to certain fullness of life."[20] Such constraint is necessary, as suggested earlier, for hope itself to exist, because, as Marcel states it, "the less life is experienced as a captivity, the less the soul will be able to see the shining of that veiled, mysterious light, which . . . illumines the very center of hope's dwelling place."[21] From Marcel's perspective, hope is born out of experience itself—the experience of travail.

His description of hope is of an ongoing process, a way of being, that ebbs and flows as one's life unfolds. He asks, "Does not the hope of the invalid, the prisoner, or the exile boil down in the end to a sort of organic refusal to accept an intolerable situation as final?"[22] In the midst of such a state of affairs, according to Marcel,

> he who hopes, inasmuch as his hope is real and not to be reduced to a mere platonic wish, seems to himself to be involved in some kind of a process; and it is only from this point of view that it is possible to realize what is specific, and, I should add super-rational, perhaps also super-relational, in hope. For, to use once again the expression I have so often employed, hope is a mystery and not a problem.[23]

Marcel, from his Christian existentialist perspective, sees the human experience—dealing with the human condition—as the ground, the very seedbed, of hope. This experience becomes transcendent as humans face their own captivity and discover that in the human condition there is "a certain vital and spiritual order which we cannot violate without exposing ourselves to the loss, not only of equilibrium, but even our integrity."[24]

Hope has its opposite in despair, the real experience of an adoptee who meets so many brick walls in the search for history, self-understanding, and care. But it is only in facing the harsh, sometimes painful realities of our lives that we are able to deal with them and transcend them. Often we discover hope in the very jaws of despair. For example, Marcel often cites the difficulty of facing an incurable illness, hearing the doctor's negative report, and refusing to accept it, not in the sense of denial (which is avoidance) but in the sense of maintaining that "a certain margin is left for me" because of the ever-possible possibility of contradiction because "it was someone else and not I who declared my recovery impossible."[25]

Marcel offers a useful contribution to the idea of hope as a theological concept by way of his ongoing interest in its metaphysical dimensions. In his definition of hope as a "transcendent act" he seeks to push the boundaries of human experience into the world of the spiritual, the communal, the realm of God. Of hope, he writes:

[W]e might say that hope is essentially the availability of a soul which has
entered intimately enough into the experience of communion to accomplish in the teeth of will and knowledge *the transcendent act*.[26]

Marcel sees the courageous, honest human being as the person who will
persevere, who will deal with every obstacle that comes along on the way
to transcendence. Living within the lights and the shadows of life is a spiritual challenge, and, for Marcel, hoping is facing that challenge by connecting to God. He calls for trust in God, not as the one who always delivers
but as one whose design may be unknowable and demanding, yet nevertheless *there*. Hope, then, is grounded in "transcendent acts," the moments
in life when human beings reach beyond the limitations of the day, and,
with teeth bared in determination, reach for the light, for a ghost parent,
for God.

Keeping hope alive is a daily activity for adoptees, especially young
adoptees who are trying, as best they can, to make sense of their experience
of being relinquished and adopted. The existential *angst* around grieving,
identity formation, creating closeness, and resolving ghost parent fantasies
is the arena in which adoptees can both hope and despair. It can be the
ground for giving up the challenge to live a full life because of disadvantage,
or it can be the ground for doing battle with negativity. The task of fighting
inwardly and outwardly for victory over shame and self-doubt and societal
discrimination can become the very basis for hoping. As one small victory
leads to another, adoptees can take hope for a better future because, even as
they are *living* in the midst of the struggle for their own souls as persons,
they may discover that the experience of fighting for themselves and for their
rights makes life meaningful. Experience becomes basis for hope along with
the hopeful realities of the past and the untold stories of the future.

Lynch's Images of Hope

William F. Lynch, a Roman Catholic priest who spent much of his life
in pastoral work with the mentally ill, has called hope

the fundamental knowledge and feeling that there is a way out of difficulty, that things can work out, that we as human persons can somehow
handle and manage internal and external reality, that there are 'solutions'
in the most ordinary biological and physiological sense of that word, that,
above all, there are ways out of illness.[27]

Building on Marcel's work, Lynch reflects on the manner in which human
experience, the painful human experience of the mentally ill, is a struggle
with hope. In his pastoral work with people in despair, people who believe

that there is "no exit," people who have given up hope, Lynch says that he discovered that mental illness and hopelessness go hand in hand. Although this correlation ought *not* mean that losing hope means that one is necessarily becoming mentally ill, it is instructive as a way to appreciate the essence of hope, not only from a psychological and emotional perspective, but also and ultimately from a theological and metaphysical perspective.

Lynch consistently makes a case for grounding hope in human experience. Specifically, he argues throughout *Images of Hope* that human reality is the source of hope, echoing the often-made comment that "reality is the best defense." Lynch asserts that reality is of one unified, coherent whole and that it stands as a solid foundation for the activity of hoping:

> There would be little reason for hope and much reason for hopelessness if reality were constructed on basically conflictual lines, in such a way, that is, that if one absolutely necessary human goal were reached another would have to be lost. Then we could not have any good thing without tragedy or without illness. . . . Here both theology and the new mental sciences are in agreement. In his very act of being master of the world God communicates his autonomy and freedom to men [sic]. He has not created an either/or world. He has not created a world where we must absolutize either of two contraries.[28]

Lynch's view of reality is that it is *not* ultimately conflictual. Instead he ascribes to "what may be called an organic or structural or integrated view of reality."[29] Being immersed in reality, belonging to it, provides the foundation for the beginning of hopefulness for all human beings, despite what may be the very difficult circumstances of everyday life, including the circumstances of relinquishment and adoption. From this perspective Lynch proceeds to illuminate how specific human experiences carry hope intrinsically. They are "images" of being hopeful, of taking on the demons of life that would wrest hope from our hands and hearts. They are imagination, mutuality, wishing, and waiting—common pieces of the adoptee experience.

Imagination

Lynch describes the creative energy in the process of imagining as the life force that constructs hope. Those who cannot imagine, in his view, cannot hope. Specifically, those who are mentally ill are so, in part, because they cannot imagine. Such a person is trapped in a limited view of reality and, therefore, unable to see or imagine what might be out there. Another's imagination is needed to begin the work of rediscovering one's own.[30] According to Lynch, the capacity to imagine, to bring to mind a vision, a mental picture, of something or someone not yet in reality, but nevertheless *thought of*, is the beginning of hope.

[O]ne of the permanent meanings of imagination has been that it is the gift that envisions what cannot yet be seen, the gift that constantly proposes to itself that the boundaries of the possible are wider than they seem. Imagination, if it is in prison and has tried every exit, does not panic or move into apathy but sits down to try to envision another way out. It is always slow to admit that all the facts are in, that all the doors have been tried, and that it is defeated. . . . It is not overcome by the absoluteness of the present moment.[31]

For most adoptees imagination is a quiet, personal place of hopefulness as they mentally play with images of ghost parents. The rich reports of birth parent fantasies, of possible reunions for some "when they grow up," of ongoing and deep connection to these missing pieces of their lives all compose a testimony, by Lynch's way of thinking, to how hopeful adoptees dare to be.

This is the power of wondering that makes imagination so central to hoping. Imagination creates perspective from the facts that it discovers. It refuses to leave these facts as absolutes that simply frighten people. It "will always suppose that there is a fact and a possibility that is not yet in."[32] The experience of adoptive development is the struggle to stay hopeful, to take in as many facts as are available and do one's best at making life work with them and without the ones kept secret. The very well-developed imaginations of adoptees keep them hoping. And such hope directs them toward a new reality that may heal and restore the empty places within themselves.

Mutuality

The second image of hope that Lynch offers has to do with the capacity for human relationship, which he calls *mutuality*.

By mutuality . . . I mean an interacting relationship, an interacting contribution between man [sic] and the world, or between person and person, or between man and God, from which something new and free is born.[33]

For Lynch, hoping that is genuine is something that is *not* done alone—by its very nature it cannot be done alone! It is not an activity so self-focused that others as others are not involved. In fact, for Lynch, others must exist in order for interiority itself to exist.[34] This relational dimension of hoping is basic to Lynch's understanding of hope and also serves to demonstrate how a relationship to God is part of hoping.

In the introduction to *Images of Hope* Lynch writes that he desires to carry the act of imagination further by insisting that it be "an act of collaboration or mutuality."[35] Genuine hope is in some way a communal activity. Hope by its very nature is a need for help, for *outside* help, well beyond the resources of the individual. Hope would not be necessary if the needed solutions to life's dilemmas resided within ourselves.

Hope cannot be achieved alone. It must in some way or other be an act of community, whether the community be a church or a nation or just two people struggling together to produce liberation in each other. People develop hope in each other, hope that they will receive help from each other. As with the imagination, we tend to always think of hope as the final act which is my own, in isolation and in self-assertion. But it is not this at all; this interpretation is, in fact, one source of its dubious and sentimentalized reputation. Hope is an act of the city of man, an act of what I call the public order, not in the external sense of that word but in the sense that it must occur between persons, whether they be man or God.[36]

The activity of hoping demands an a priori connectedness of some form, human or divine, in order for hoping itself to happen. Without this condition hopelessness invades hope and defeats it.

According to Lynch, mutuality serves as the "source of unconditionality and autonomy,"[37] two conditions that are necessary in order for hope to occur. In the safety and the acceptance of unconditionality, with the freedom that autonomy-within-relationship offers, a person is able to begin the process of hoping, of striving for the transcendence and reinterpretation of difficult experience. This being-in-relationship is so central for Lynch that without it, with the collapse of mutuality, "the world is no longer seen as bringing help,"[38] no longer on the side of hope. God is then dead. Life is then without hope.

Human beings need connection to someone outside themselves in such a way as to be and remain hopeful. Only then can they move beyond painful circumstances to a new and improved reality, not by way of interior willfulness, but by way of an inner strength derived from the creative energy that relationships can foster. For those people who have been relinquished and adopted, there are several possibilities in these terms of mutuality, different points of contact. For one, in very practical ways, adoptees gather for mutual support and encouragement in their quest to complete their life stories. Such support and advocacy groups are common in all the major metropolitan areas of America. Adoptees today do not hope alone. They have created community.

But there's more. A second point of contact may be with the person, the ghost parent, who may be hoping from the other side. There is, indeed, a connection to these lost but real people. Most often, in search and reunion stories, birth parents, especially birth mothers, testify that they were hoping all along, year after year, that news would come and hearts would mend. This sense of ghost parent connection is very much a part of hoping for adoptees, especially those in search. But most importantly, there is the relationship to God, who may act graciously in terms of human hopes. Keeping this relationship with God, which at times is in jeopardy when hope is overcome by despair, is critical to staying hopeful as days and weeks and years go by without answers to the adoptee's basic questions about self. By holding on to these relationships adoptees hold hope.

Wishing

"Where there is no wishing there can be no hope,"[39] writes Lynch, as he begins his exploration of wishing as an image of hope. He ties the two very closely together, always seeing the one in the other. Wishing, for Lynch, is the hallmark for mental well-being and spiritual health. He writes:

> Wherever I use the words *wish* or *wishing*, I wish to indicate something deeply positive. The sense is that of the *Book of Daniel*, in which the angel says to the prophet: God has loved you because you are a man of desires. We must take man [sic] as essentially a wishing, desiring being who, in this exalted sense, must at all costs be in contact with his own wishes.[40]

We, as human beings, are known by our wishes, and our deepest wishes may tell us the most about ourselves.[41] Adoptees wish, and sometimes they wish deeply, for the peace that comes with hearing their birth stories, knowing their truth, and resolving the very hidden mysteries of their lives.

Wishing, for Lynch, is also the direct road to spirituality. The deep interiority of wishing is the place where we "make contact with our souls, whether this possession be called identity by the medical man or 'salvation' by the theologian."[42] Lynch believes that our task as humans is to be deeply connected to our wishes (which he terms "absolute wishes"[43]) in order for us to be truly in communion with God. Wishing is the way, the method, by which we discern the will of God in our lives. It is in our wishes, in our yearnings, that we find God's direction for who we are to be, for what we are to do, and for the future we are to create. God wants us to wish, and in our wishes we hear the whisper of God's voice.

For Lynch, the activity of imagination occurs within the context of mutuality and is fueled by wishing. Without the wish neither of the others is effective. If a young adoptee is taught *not* to wish for the knowledge of birth parents, *not* to wish for connection to birth families, *not* to wish for truth and a full understanding of personal history; then something gets lost in terms of deeper self-knowledge and greater connection to God and greater connection to life. With wishing comes more openness and freedom to discover one's self in relation to God and to the world around us, including the world that vanished at birth or shortly thereafter. The adoptee, for example, who is in search for reunion with a missing ghost parent is on a quest that holds more promise for the future through more connection to the past. And God, the One who creates hope through human wishing, becomes more real.

Waiting

For some adoptees waiting is a word that has always characterized living. Waiting actively and waiting hopefully is sometimes a difficult watch in the long night of not knowing. Lynch speaks to the difficulties in waiting:

> The ability to wait is central to hope, and must therefore have an essential place in human wishing. If hope directs itself toward good things that belong to the future and that are often difficult to achieve, then it must know how to wait. The kind of wishing that can wait is the mark of ongoing maturity.... Two kinds of waiting must be carefully distinguished. One waits because there is nothing else to do. The other, which goes with hope, is positive and creative. It waits because it knows what it wishes and wants.[44]

Hope that is genuine demonstrates the capacity to wait, sometimes patiently, sometimes impatiently, because it is so charged with hope. Waiting is the hard part of hoping, where hope itself is constantly tested. Waiting, for Lynch, is the creative act of challenging the impossible of the present moment; of refusing to give up and cease wishing for and imagining a better future. It is the ongoing decision, remade moment after moment, that, in the face of difficulty, refuses to accede but instead transcends present circumstances and looks with an eye to the future. It is critical to hoping.

> The waiting we talk about is positive and creative; it makes real wishing possible. When properly understood and exercised it means the ability to remain fixed upon a goal, to cope with obstacles, to make detours when an immediate path is blocked, to be willing to take all the intermediate means that are essential to attaining the goal.[45]

Waiting is the behavior that demonstrates a trust that the future will somehow hold, will keep promise alive, will indeed happen in a fashion that goes well beyond the present difficulties of the day. Waiting is living for many adoptees.

A Woman of Hope

Susannah steadfastly refused to give up being hopeful—an impressive feat, given her life story. She had come for pastoral counseling after hearing a presentation on relinquishment and adoption and their relation to identity and success in life. She was thirty years old and had been married for six years. Susannah was relinquished at birth, kept in foster care for four months, and then adopted. When she was two years old her parents separated, and when she was four they divorced. (These are clearly issues of adoption, *not* of relinquishment.) She grew her with her mother and her brother, who was two years older and who physically abused her for much of her childhood. At times his beatings were severe. When she reported this abuse to her mother and stepfather, they dismissed it as untrue. For a year Susannah lived without a bedroom door; although her brother had broken it down to "get at her," she was blamed and therefore punished. She moved away to college for one year and then returned home, homesick, wanting better connections with her family. But Susannah was "thrown out of the house" at one point in response to ongoing conflict in her adoptive family.

Neither her mother nor her brother were held accountable for their abuse. Her father kept his distance and never said a word, and her stepfather believed he had no right to say anything. Susannah was alone in the conflict. Finally she just left. At the time of counseling she had not spoken to any family member for nearly a year.

Susannah presented a variety of physical symptoms that have added difficulty to her complicated life. She reported three medical conditions: Ménière's disease, hypothyroidism, and fibromyalgia. She regularly gets a massage for tight muscles in her neck. Although she is thirty, she says she has been told by several doctors that she has the body of a fifty-year-old. Her hands shake constantly, her circulation is poor, and she is always cold. She reports that she is never able to relax, as if she is traumatized, *not yet* posttraumatic. She sleeps poorly. Susannah wonders how all this relates to her miscarriage of a year ago, saying it is as if "my body will not let me have a child."

The miscarriage triggered Susannah's search for her birth parents. Because her birth mother had signed up with a voluntary state registry ten years earlier, the search was completed in three weeks. (The registry was in the building next door to the one where Susannah had worked for six years.) Susannah had hopes of making her upcoming reunion go well.

In thinking about her life experience, both before and after reunion, Susannah wrote pages and pages of first-person narrative for our review. Here are several of her reflections:

> Like an infant, with total dependence, full trust, frank openness, and complete sincerity, I have always seen myself in terms of the larger deeper picture: the Circle of life, the divine plan of God (the father), and of (mother) Nature. As a little girl, I had always felt the deep detachment and isolation, separation and loss of adoption [relinquishment?] that set me apart from others. My equilibrium was out of balance. Funny, I should suffer from a debilitating balance disorder: Ménière's disease. Funny, that it should affect my hearing, as I have heard the unimaginable out of the mouths of my family, both families even. I no longer trust in these senses for use in this physical world, I trust in my intuition that I use in My world, the spiritual world of relinquishment and adoption.

Detachment, at such an early and fragile age, for me, involved intense concentration and reflection inward. Immeasurable effort was spent to acquire the ability to rise above my pain and suffering, knowing that I had no destination and that anything was possible, and would be better than the excruciating pain of the present. What I was experiencing had no words or name, and many times, as a child, my lack of understanding kept me from crying tears at what I had lost.

As an adopted child, I did not know where I "fit in" and belonged, in the smaller picture. In the reality of my world, the larger picture, what kept me from "fitting in" was the fact that I have always seen, and felt, and blindly known myself to be filled with infinite potential, a concept not well known in the physical world. My seed was going to bloom and grow in any soil that Nature proved. I was, and am, the set and the sum of all possibilities: my biology unknown, I therefore am not limited by it, or much else for that matter.

I will probably never know and fully understand the impact of human love, the love that a child feels when its mother holds, loves, and nurtures the first days of their life and young soul. That love that grows day by day and carries forward—even after your parents have passed on. I recall so few times in childhood when I was held, truly held, so that the warmth of a gentle embrace and the touching of a nose or cheek to mine would light a fire to warm the cold of darkness in my world. But I will have and know the enormous impact of God's love and grace. However, puzzling as it is, here on Earth, Love has never been "enough." We've always sought and looked, and even needed so much more.

Susannah's reunion with her birth mother, a neonatal neurologist, was a mixed experience. It might have gone better if Susannah had expected less. Her birth mother had relinquished Susannah in order to pursue studies toward medical school. In Susannah's own words, she was "not important enough to be kept." She let her birth mother know in no uncertain terms that that was how she felt. She was clear in her request for a deeper commitment to each other. "Friends" was not good enough. She wanted to be part of her birth mother's family, which included a fourteen-year-old half brother. Susannah asked for the name of her birth father in order to pursue reunion with him. Her birth mother refused. On the occasion of their first meeting (a thousand miles away from Susannah's home) Susannah was dropped off at the airport several hours early. Her birth mother had had enough. It appeared that Susannah had jeopardized the future of her connection to her birth mother by asking so quickly for so much. Unless there would be substantial gain in their relationship, Susannah could not take the risk of relating. In effect she reexperienced her relinquishment, in that her birth mother had seemingly "really let go." This reopened the wound for Susannah, and it hurt too much to stay too close. A tragedy of sorts. The care that her birth mother could offer, which was not nearly as much as Susannah demanded, was shut away. Again, Susannah was once again alone.

Obviously, Susannah's retreat to her hope-filled "spiritual world" of relinquishment and adoption served a necessary defensive purpose. There was no other "safe place to be" for much of her life. Her own experience of God was in this *nonphysical* world where no one could be relinquished or abused. In her "spiritual world" she found the needed safety from all the pain. Her body had some of the pain, manifested in a variety of chronic symptoms. Her mind had disconnected, moving away from hurtful people in a dissociative fashion. Her heart, carefully protected, seemed chronically broken. Life was not mending for Susannah. She stayed in her "spiritual world" for all these reasons. She kept her faith in God, her hope that the future could still be good . . . even if no one else came through, even if her birth parents gave her up, even if her adoptive parents left each other and her as well, even if her brother beat her, and even if her life felt incomplete and unfulfilling.

Despite days of discouragement, Susannah remained hopeful. Yes, she employed defenses that we would tend to pathologize: depression, anxiety, dissociation (symptoms of posttraumatic stress), splitting people into only good and bad. Yes, she retreated from reality. But given the fracturing of her life into twos—relinquishment and adoption, birth parents and adoptive parents, her brother's beatings and longed-for relief, the real world of pain and the spiritual world of fantasy—God was understandably positioned in a safe place, the realm of experience beyond the reach of injury. Her God was accessible by retreat, not through community, but by leaving community. Certainly, how much God can exist for Susannah in the real world, in everyday life with people, remains an open question. Nevertheless, hope kept Susannah going. God still existed, even if "protected from review" in her spiritual world. The Spirit of God speaks *within* the depression, *within* the anxiety, *within* the "friend" called dissociation, and *within* the need to order one's world into black and white categories.

What remains for Susannah is to hear the voice of God's Spirit in her birth mother's decision to register ten years earlier in order to be found, in her adoptive mother's weak attempts to care for her daughter, in her husband's effort to make life good for her, and in the "news" that, indeed, relinquishment is a primal wound that needs mending, not a story to be forgotten. Susannah's stubborn refusal to let life defeat her comes from keeping hope alive. She hopes that she will discover the depth of care and the reality of personal significance that will carry her forward to a better day. To some important degree her hope can make her whole.

Keeping Hope in Check

As odd as it may sound, it is also important not to be too hopeful. Adoptees know about this. In the study of birth parent fantasies discussed in chapter 5 it was noted that several respondents were quite aware of stopping their fantasies because they did not want to be too hopeful, lest the pain of never knowing and never meeting be too intense. There is a fine line between being hopeful and not daring to be too hopeful, but both are significant parts of adoptive experience. Keeping hope in check means taking caution not to walk on ice that may be too thin, not pressing hope beyond the boundaries of what might be reasonable to expect, not imagining that your birth parents will indeed show up and take you home. When much is at stake, being careful, playing things "close to the vest," may be wise.

And much may be at stake. Like a moth circling too close to the floodlight, adoptees are sometimes burned. When Eliza knocked on the door of her birth father's condominium, knowing full well that he was on the other side of the one-inch wall of pine, her heart was in her throat. She hoped. She wanted so much for him to acknowledge her as a person, a daughter, his daughter. For thirty-eight years the secret had been kept. The sealed records had made the search difficult. Missouri state law kept the file shut. If only this door would open, so many things would be different. If only this man would be honest with himself and with Eliza that she was indeed his offspring. If only truth could be told and accepted and even embraced. If only this door would open.

But it did not. Her heart sank, and her face turned stone cold. The scuffling on the other side continued the saga of secrecy. It was the sound of someone hiding, hiding from truth, hiding from responsibility, hiding from relationship, and hiding from the goodness of care. So, understandably, Eliza was careful not to be too hopeful. Perhaps in that moment she had hoped too much. She had to learn, once again, that sometimes people, important people, do not come through, do not care, and do not do what is right. In this light, *hoping can be dangerous because it puts the human heart at risk*. And when the risk has to do with future development, with a sense of well-being, and with the belief that God does care, then so much is at stake that it is dangerous to be too hopeful and jeopardize those good things.

When relationships run out of hope they die, but if one puts too much hope in unfulfilled relationships they stay alive in a fashion that may be barely tolerable. It is a matter of proportion, of dosage in terms of how much hope is manageable for the adoptee. It is deciding daily how much to reach for the stars when the evening sky is cloudy, when the future looms with the potential dread of feeling an old wound again. Keeping balance between hope and despair, between believing and disbelieving in the care of ghost parents, between trusting God and keeping a "safe" distance from God is the ongoing task. The sanity of adoptees may depend on how much they dare to be hopeful, and sometimes that includes keeping hope in check.

Hope as Hearing the Voice of God

Lynch argues in *Images of Hope* that all of what goes on in hoping is first of all and finally spiritual. His ongoing concern is what he calls the "loss of the soul,"[46] and, therefore, the loss of relationship to God. This connection is vital. "We can get along without our soul for a little while in life," he writes, "but not for long."[47] Hope is ultimately about our stance before God, our "position" with regard to the Divinity, however God be defined. The person who hopes well, who keeps hope alive, who refuses defeat in the face of difficulty, this person, according to Lynch, stands well before God in relationship to God. The person who hopes is one who draws upon "the healing power of existence and reality"[48] in such a way as to be spiritually whole. Hoping is about the awareness of God in our lives, specifically of God's grace. He writes:

> The generic meaning of grace is that of some help communicated from the outside, from God, to man [sic]. A still more precise meaning is that it is above all the demands and expectations of human nature, that is given *gratis* by God, for no other reason than he wishes to. One of the most splendid qualities of the outside world, whether that world be things or God or a teacher or a parent or a doctor, is the ability to communicate help in such a way as to create in others the interior ability to really wish.[49]

So, when we wish and wish deeply for the things that matter to us, including our connections to people of importance, whether for mates of tomorrow or friends of today or ghost parents of yesterday, we are attending to the voice of God, who whispers in our ears the names of people who are important. Adoptees want to know the names so that they can keep on hoping.

A child begins life "full of hope that everything in life, every object, every person, will conform to the security of certain ideal moments spent with a mother acting ideally in terms of his needs. This is the first dream of hope."[50] Obviously, this reference touches upon the profound importance of connection with a *birth* mother, a bond that is broken in the process of extrafamilial adoption. It is this primal injury that may feed a sense of hopelessness in relinquished and adopted persons. The painful reality of this early-life rejection, remembered or not, depending upon the age of a child, is a heavy stone to carry, a moment in time difficult to transcend. But with hope transcending it becomes possible. As Gabriel Marcel puts it:

> We might say that if time is in its essence a separation and, as it were, a perpetual splitting up of the self in relation to itself, hope on the contrary aims at reunion, at recollection, at reconciliation: in that way, and in that way alone, it might be called a *memory of the future (italics added)*.[51]

Along the road of the adoptee's journey hope remains, not hidden in Pandora's box and unavailable to humankind, but alive and beating in the hearts of adoptees.

Chapter Seven

Adoptees and God:
A Variety of Images

I was never very close to God in the first place. But when I got into therapy and started to deal with all this adoption stuff, I felt like I was losing God.

—Patricia, age forty-three

She walked slowly and shyly into the counseling office, carefully clutching an old paper bag.[1] Despite her physical maturity, her steps were those of a young child as she moved toward her chair and sat down. After eleven months of pastoral counseling she at last had found the courage to present this piece of her personal history to me. Patricia quietly opened the paper bag that she held protectively and lifted out a ragged scrapbook that showed its thirty-nine years. With tears streaming down both cheeks she opened this tattered window to her past, turning to a page where a little girl's tarnished gold bracelet lay taped to the fragile paper. Although it would no longer fit her wrist, in a poignant and powerful way she was still wearing it. This tarnished little bracelet was the only link to her origins that Patricia owned.

As the process of pastoral counseling unfolded, this relinquished and adopted woman regularly reported that she was afraid that she was "losing God." Her carefully controlled world, which included a polished, affect-free exterior, was caving in. Her relationship with her adoptive parents, now elderly, was plagued with distance and difficulty. She was one of eight adopted children, the quiet one who felt lost in the crowd. A major depression had taken over her life and had deeply affected both her marriage and her relationship to one of her three adopted sons. What had worked for forty years of her life was no longer working. Antidepressant medications had only taken the edge off her inner suffering. Patricia was coming to life in a very painful but important way. Fully aware that she would never be the same person again, she held her childhood bracelet to her heart and wept, wondering why she had been relinquished.

Paradise may quickly be lost for relinquished and adopted children. Regardless of how well the process of adoption is managed, a real rejection occurs. This, as we have seen, is a sting that may be felt in childhood with the dawning of awareness about what relinquishment means, as well as in adult life, when the questions around relinquishment linger like a cloud of mystery over the heads of the wondering. Adoptees, unlike the rest of us, face questions about God unique to their experience of being relinquished. How do children of adoption design their perceptions of God in the light of their lived experience? How do they think about God? How do they feel about God? It may well be that placing an infant or a young child like Patricia in a home with substitute parents has a significant impact on the development of her understanding and experience of God. That possibility is the focus of this chapter.

Part of human awareness is wondering about one's origins and one's destiny. For adoptees these questions may take on a sense of *in*security. Steven L. Nickman points this out in an article entitled "Losses in Adoption":

> We all wonder where we came from and how we will meet our end; these are the primary questions from which religion and philosophy spring. How do we contemplate a past in which we played no part and a future which will proceed without us? Blood ties attenuate the pain of these questions for most people; adoptees, however, are brought closer to a sense of *basic anxiety* about their place in the world.[2]

How might this basic anxiety, this *angst* of relinquishment, play itself out in the development and use of the adoptee's image of God? Patricia was rightly concerned that she knew nothing about either of her birth parents. The precious bracelet was a gift from a foster father who had put together a "life book" for her on the occasion of her placement into her adoptive family, at age three and a half. Her thoughts about *both* her birth parents and her (very loving) foster parents were filled with questions about the many possible motivations for not keeping her. In the process of pastoral counseling she allowed herself to reexperience her early losses by pushing people away; she especially pushed away her husband and one of her sons. (And, of course, her pastoral counselor.) But she also pushed God away. At times the Almighty was nowhere to be found.

The Concept of God—Psychologically Speaking

Where does the concept of God come from in a child's world of personal representations? From the perspective of psychoanalytic thought a person's God-concept, his or her way of thinking of God, is a construct formed from infantile parental images. Early self-object and object representations (experiences of people as *part* of the self and experiences of people as *other* than the self) become the grist for the construction of God representations in the face of both joys and vulnerabilities. However, in contrast to Freud's proposal that God is simply the vestige of infantile wishes, God representations may be seen as being formed and usefully reformed as life proceeds into adulthood. This means that a person's concept of God usually changes as life goes on. For adoptees like Patricia, the construction, deconstruction, and reconstruction of a particular image of God may have unusual twists and turns because of the dilemmas that relinquishment presents.

Rizzuto's Images of the Living God

Ana-Maria Rizzuto puts a very positive face on God representations from her own psychoanalytic perspective. She writes that "it is out of the matrix of facts and fantasies, wishes, hopes, and fears, in the exchange with these incredible beings called parents, that the image of God is concocted."[3] In contrast Freud,[4] who believed that a God representation is simply the (unfortunate) projection of childhood wishes, Rizzuto sees positive psychological utility in the development and nurture of one's private representation of God "during childhood and [with] its modifications and uses during the entire course of life."[5] She regards a person's God representation as

> a *new* original representation which, because it is new, may have the varied components that serve to soothe and comfort, provide inspiration and courage—or terror and dread—far beyond that inspired by the actual parents.[6]

According to Rizzuto, we develop our images of God, our mental pictures about the who and the what of the Divine, from our first experiences in life with parents or caregivers. These people have the most to do with our approach to spiritual dimensions of our lives. And, as we relate to parents by way of our representations of them, so we also relate to what we experience as divine by way of our God representations. We employ these concepts as a method of connecting. They assist in our efforts to answer our questions about the nature of God and to find a way to relate to God.

This mental creation of a God representation, a new object/being that is beyond the scope of reality testing, is part of life experience. In Rizzuto's view, it makes us "psychologically viable people in the real world."[7] Given this "birth of the living God" in the child's mind, Rizzuto concludes that experiencing this God representation plays an important role in the psychic life of every individual, *regardless of whether or not God is consciously believed in*. She posits that "once formed, the representation of God is given all the psychic potentials of a living person who is nonetheless experienced only in the privacy of conscious and unconscious processes."[8] Shaping and reshaping this psychic construct is part of life. It serves the ongoing functions of maintaining mental health and developing a spiritual/theological perspective for each of us, once again, regardless of the specific content that we may give to it.

Now, consider the dilemma of Patricia and other relinquished and adopted people with regard to the creation of God representations. The adoptee's construction of parent representations, the alleged grist of images of God, has been a task fraught with conflict and corresponding ambivalence. The double-representational world of the adoptee includes a continuum of positive to negative parental representations, some of which are "born" in the midst of significant suffering as they relate to primal rejection. Only limited constructive use can be made of parental representations that may elicit memory traces or notions of rejection and abandonment. (Despite years of church going, Patricia reported that while she was growing up she could "only barely believe in God.") The construction of images of God that are benevolent and caring may serve useful defensive functions in terms of preserving psychic equilibrium, especially in times of stress. However, for some adoptees, these positive notions of God may not be available because the pain of facing early rejection may be too overwhelming for the ego to manage. Some adoptee believers may maintain primitive, even infantile formulations of God representations which remain fixated, stuck in time as objects of awe. Or, more consistent with their early experience, some adoptee nonbelievers, sounding like Patricia, may reject both birth parent representations and God representations as equally unacceptable for exaltation.[9]

Kohut's Bipolar Self

Heinz Kohut, in his development of the psychology of the self, has expanded psychoanalytic theory to include a careful review of what he calls self-object relationships. (*Object* means person in the language of psychological theory and *self-object* refers to a particular use of a person as an extension of the self.) Kohut posits the *self* as a fourth psychic structure in a separate line of development alongside the tripartite Freudian construction of id, ego, superego. This self is the experience-near center of an individual's universe. The self, as it relates to its self-object and object representational world, is "bipolar," meaning that it functions both by making assignments of importance to one's self (which he calls "grandiosity") and by making assignments of significance to others (which Kohut calls "idealization"). These he considers ongoing, concurrent functions of the self which serve as an attempt to maintain the "original perfection" of the merger between the infant and the caregiver. Both are avenues toward ways in which God can be experienced.

When the self of the infant, in response to breaks in empathy from the primary caregiver, makes assignments of self-importance, Kohut calls this "the grandiose self."[10] In this scenario, the infant seeks the mirroring of others in order to maintain internal cohesion. Mirroring has to do with attending to the emotional needs of the child by admiring and caring for the child, mirroring back the goodness of the baby with a smile. Everything is OK as long as the child is noticed. This ongoing noticing and caring is critical to the healthy development of the self. When, however, this mirroring is lost, as may be in the case with relinquishment and the awkwardness of beginning adoption, the self of the infant/child may be stuck in the needing stage and be unable to gradually moderate narcissistic needs and become more accepting of the mirroring that people can realistically offer.

Given this developmental scenario, the experience of God for some has much to do with the sense of significance that comes from being noticed. You may not think about God much when you have some notion that "you are God," that others ought to "worship" you, at least in the early years of life. But this is the position that each of us takes to some degree in our beginnings. (Ask any mother about the grocery store tantrums we threw as children when we did not get our way!) This is the birthplace of our own self-esteem, our sense of worthiness as persons—the origins of believing in ourselves that translates into a sense of well-being in adult life. Without sufficient mirroring *all* of us lose a sense of personal importance. For the grandiose part of the self, according to Kohut, there is an ongoing need for admiration in order for anyone to be a fully functional adult. And the experience may include the belief that God's face shines on *us*. The idea that God's blessings come *our* way, that we are to be treated well by the Divine, that God mirrors *us* in our daily living—this is the goodness of a mirroring God.

With regard to the process of the idealization of others, Kohut outlines a process of development that may correlate with the construction of another concept of God. He explains that

> the psyche saves a part of the lost experience of global narcissistic perfection by assigning it to an archaic, rudimentary (transitional) self-object, the idealized parent imago. Since all bliss and power now reside in the idealized object, the child feels empty and powerless when he is separated from it and he attempts, therefore, to maintain a continuous union with it.[11]

Out of a sense of emptiness and vulnerability from (understandable) breaks in empathy by caregivers comes another attempt to salvage the psychic day by believing that another (the *idealized parent imago*[12]) holds all the perfection needed to keep things calm. The fledgling ego of the child assigns wonder and greatness to another person/being in order to maintain the cohesion of the self, to avoid fragmentation and its resulting despair, and to thereby save the goodness that life may have.

Kohut notes specifically how the loss of a parent, consistent with the early experience of adoptees, may complicate psychological development.

> In the specific case of the traumatic loss of the idealized parent imago (loss of the idealized self-object or disappointment in it) up to and including the Oedipal phase [through age four or five], the results are disturbances in the specific narcissistic sectors of the personality. Under optimal circumstances the child experiences gradual disappointment in the idealized object—or, expressed differently: the child's evaluation of the idealized object becomes increasingly realistic. . . . If the child suffers the traumatic loss of the idealized object, however, or a traumatic (severe and sudden, or not phase-appropriate) disappointment in it, then optimal internalization does not take place. The child does not acquire the needed internal structure, his psyche remains fixated on an archaic self-object, and the personality will throughout life be dependent on certain objects in what seems to be an intense form of object hunger. The intensity of the search for and of the dependency on these objects is due to the fact that they are striven for as a substitute for the missing segments of the psychic structure [of the self].[13]

In response to the pain of loss, there are certain ways by which the human mind seeks repair. When the needed idealized parent/person is suddenly no longer available as a resource for coping, it is possible this narcissistic injury interferes with development by leaving the child empty and needy, and without ongoing necessary emotional nurture from others. Then certain defenses against that pain may be set in motion.

There are two developmental steps in which this construction of the "idealized parent imago" may relate directly to the God representations of relinquished and adopted children. First, depending on the age of the child, this idealized self-object/being may be created in the mind of the adoptee in order, in part, to *compensate* unconsciously for the initial loss of self—experienced in the historical event of relinquishment. The human psyche makes something up because something hurts. Second, when cognitive awareness of relinquishment dawns, as described in chapter 2, this narcissistic injury may demand *fixation* at a point of limited emotional development. To proceed with the de-idealization of the self-object/being (even if it is no longer available) may be just too painful and, accordingly, the adoptee, now aware of his or her own abandonment, may remain fixated on the object/birth parent "as is." Kohut alerts us to a lifelong process of development, a lifelong need for people and things and places to function as self-objects in our lives. These continuously calm narcissistic needs and translate into movement from a childlike belief in a great mother-father-God imago to a much more modulated appreciation for one's participation in something/someone much more powerful than any of us here on Earth, which Kohut calls "cosmic narcissism."

In the midst of this rather complicated understanding of psychological development we consider the adoptee, once again, looking for God. But the movement from primitive God representations toward more mature understandings of the (divine) mirroring parent or the idealized parent image may be hampered by the conflict and ambivalence that are part of the adoptee's double-representational world. Put differently, the need to be admired or to idealize in response to the unacceptable imperfections of parental figures in the adoptee's early life may be so intense as to preclude the growth that is necessary in the narcissistic sectors of personality, that is, where a healthy sense of self and self-esteem takes root (the grandiose self) and where we form our ideals and ambitions for living. In that case, God representations will remain fixed at a certain point, or, if further traumatic injury occurs in the forced breakdown of idealized images (e.g., adoptive parents who do not honor the role of the birth parents), God representations may be rejected or repressed. If so, then the adoptee, unable to connect to something or someone warm and wonderful, is left to conclude that "I hate God" or to ask Patricia's question: "Is there a God at all?"

God Representations—Theologically Speaking

Extrafamilial adoption begins, as we have seen, with an experience of rejection, of not being allowed to fit in the world where one began. It is also the experience of being received, accepted, and taken in by others who commit to care. The adoptee is given a new name, a new status, a new place in the world. The theological accuracy of the adoptee's God representations depends on how the journey goes from the first home to the second, from being "abandoned to the world" to being claimed by new parents. Developing an understanding of God that fits God depends on how the adoptee is able to *deal* with relinquishment in the context of the care of the adoptive home . . . because relinquishment may challenge faith.

Tillich's Courage to Be

The existentially focused theology of Paul Tillich, especially as presented in *The Courage to Be*, offers a description of spiritual struggle that may be useful in understanding the spiritual dilemma of the adoptee. We begin with his definition of courage:

> Courage is the affirmation of one's essential nature, one's inner aim . . . , but it also an affirmation which has in itself the character of "in spite of." It includes the possible and, in some cases, the unavoidable sacrifice of elements which also belong to one's being, but which, if sacrificed, would prevent us from reaching our actual fulfillment.[14]

These words speak precisely to the dilemma of the relinquished and adopted child, specifically as they relate to the sacrifice of birth parents and birth history. Living as a relinquished and adopted person means becoming a person "in spite of" how difficult the start was. Tillich's comment is meant to describe courage as something that each of us uses in taking on and dealing with the brokenness of "nonbeing" in its many forms. Relinquishment, the breaking of a relationship, is only one form; however, it serves as a powerful example of an occasion in life where the "courage to be," the courage to be a unique person in spite of being put off by parents, is essential in order for a child to move along in the development of a useful understanding of God.

Tillich offers a foundation for the importance of courage to be. He delineates the spiritual struggle of all of humankind to come to terms with an understanding of God, "the fundamental symbol of our ultimate concern."[15] He writes that struggling with one's ultimate concern "gives depth, direction, and unity to all other concerns, and, with them, to the whole personality."[16] His method is that of an existential analysis of the human condition. He focuses on the manner in which we all seek to derive meaning from our daily existence, especially in the light of the trials and adversities of living. His thoughts are directly relevant to the existential crisis in which adoptees may find themselves, namely that of having the biohistorical genetics of one family and the personal-emotional experience of another. How this drama plays itself out theologically in an adoptee's appropriation of an understanding of God is our immediate concern.

When Patricia entered pastoral psychotherapeutic treatment, her God, as she understood God, had failed her. She had grown up being taught a concept of God as a loving, benevolent, personal deity who gave favor to all human beings "who believed." But this idea of God did not square with the growing awareness of her own abandonment and feelings of despair. For Patricia, entering life meant entering the death of this concept of God. What she had been taught all her life did not ring true. God, as she was taught to think about God, seemed quite unavailable. God may have been there in a different way, but it was not working for her. She depended on antidepressant medications to get through each day of her busy life with her family.

The method of psychodynamically oriented psychotherapy has to do with finding out what one does not want to know, with turning one's head toward whatever one has turned away from. When Patricia tearfully hung on to the tarnished bracelet of her childhood in the counseling session, she also began to consider the possibility that God could be thought of in a new and different way, not simply as an imagined parental image who nourishes and protects, but rather as one who engages us in the midst of personal suffering and calls forth our own unknown strengths. Further counseling led to her decision to participate in a new worshiping community that understood God differently. As Patricia moved emotionally from one set of (adoptive) parents who had used her and her siblings on the farm as much as they had cared for her, toward another set (the ghost/foster parents) who had left her years ago but possibly still cared about her now in her adult life, she also moved from one theological understanding of God to another. Embracing her tarnished little bracelet was the beginning of rebirth.

The experience of God is, for Tillich, this embracing experience; the experience of facing reality, becoming more aware of the truth that we only partially dare to know about ourselves and our experience. Escaping God, refusing to acknowledge our own nakedness, as in the Garden of Eden, is always the temptation. Quite understandably, it may be especially difficult to affirm oneself as an adoptee when doing so means facing the sacrifice of lost ghost parents. The struggles around relinquishment, as we have seen, may be painful. But to struggle, to call things the way they are, is the beginning of facing God. As an adoptee, denial or lack of self-affirmation may mean conceiving of a god smaller than God who has left the adoptee homeless, alone in a world of strangers. God, then, is a god who abandons. From Tillich's perspective, adoptees really encounter the God beyond God (his term for the god beyond the God of traditional theism) only when they begin to accept the painful losses of their lives, only when valued ghost parents are honestly mourned. This would be spiritually affirming, the beginning of spiritual self-affirmation, Patricia's opportunity to be born again.

For Tillich, anxiety is part of life. But when special conditions prevent a person from facing the real (existential) anxiety of everyday life, then mental illness, and, for our purposes, spiritual malaise, result. When the idea of God as a caring, benevolent deity is not appropriated because suffering in early life leaves a person blind to God's being, then the very resource that is needed for spiritual imagination and refreshment is not available. This may be the spiritual dilemma of some adoptees; if God is not *experienced* as being available as a caring, interested parental figure, then where does the adoptee go for spiritual strength and hope for the future?

Tillich's definition of neurosis is interesting: "the way of avoiding nonbeing by avoiding being."[17] These terms are especially fitting for adoptees. Nonbeing, as Tillich employs the word, refers to the ongoing threat that each of us deals with to *not* live life to its fullest, to avoid the parts of our selves that are touched with pain and therefore tender to the touch. "We don't go there," so to speak, at least not easily. Nonbeing, for the adoptee, may be a good term to describe the situation of relinquishment in which there is part of the person that is "not being," unless kept in fantasy or lifted into awareness by the encouragement of a sensitive adoptive parent. Otherwise, there is part of the adoptee's self that just does not "be," is not honored and affirmed, but rather is denied the reality of being. And then, to avoid the pain of such nonbeing, adoptees may also avoid being; they are *not* (like most of us are not) all that they could be.

Tillich sees all of humankind struggling with a basic sense of disconnection from both self and others. Although we have been careful to note the distinctiveness of the relinquishment-adoption experience, here we see that all of us have something in common with the adoptee, namely the rupture of relationships with other people and with God. "[U]nder [these] conditions of human finitude and estrangement," Tillich writes, "that which is essentially united becomes essentially split."[18] We become separated from ourselves and others and we employ all kinds of methods, like making believe that it does not matter, to maintain the split. Tillich agrees with Calvin that "the human mind . . . is a permanent factory of idols" as well as "a permanent factory of fears—the first in order to escape God, the second in order to escape anxiety."[19] In a very poignant way the adoptee is anxious, *left* at a very deep level, the very place where belief in God becomes a possibility.

For Tillich, to be human is to be estranged in some way from others and from God. The adoptee faces a particular form of estrangement in being cut off from real living birth parents who appear to be attending to their own lives, *without concern* for the child that was "given up" for adoption. Painful words. It may be that such conflicted images of parents become the grist for representations of God which are similarly conflicted. The theology of relinquished and adopted children may be organized to some degree around estrangement from parents, and therefore from God, as the original state of spiritual affairs.

Tillich warns against the loss of self through lack of self-affirmation:

> It is the danger of loss of self which elicits the protest against them [resistances to being] and gives rise to the courage to be as oneself—a courage which is threatened by the loss of the world.[20]

These words are written in the context of his comments about the importance of uncompromised participation in the world for all of us. His point is that finding the courage to be oneself is a formidable task, considering all the pressures in the world to conform. Hearing God means participating, perhaps following the sound of a dissonant echo, with courage. However, it is exactly here where adoptees may be at significant disadvantage in terms of starting out in life with a depleted self. Although all of us struggle with God in different ways, the challenge for adoptees to live a life filled with meaning may be the struggle to bring the nonbeing that relinquishment creates, with all of its ghosts, into the being of full participation in living as a four-parent person.

For Tillich, there is a way toward self-affirmation, toward the experience of God. It is the way of grace. The power to affirm oneself is a gift; it is *charis*, not so much an action as a moment of reception.

> One cannot command the courage to be and one cannot give it by obey-ing a command. Religiously speaking, it is a matter of grace.[21]

This is the experience of "the power of acceptance," the antidote for the personal pain that adoptees may know in relinquishment. But it is *not* a pulling-of-the-bootstraps activity, not a work, not an accomplishment. *It is God that acts.* It is the moment of meeting and knowing the "God beyond God" in the midst of the diminishment and shame that children of adop-tion may experience emotionally and spiritually. In Patricia's story the pas-toral counseling relationship became a *means* of grace whereby she was able to begin the process of self-affirmation and restoration toward becoming what Tillich calls the "New Being."

In Tillich's words, this is the moment of "being grasped by one's ulti-mate concern." This experiential something—being grasped, becoming aware, like the prodigal son of Luke 15 who "came unto himself"—is given meaning as of ultimate concern. The adoptee, at some time, is in the midst of being grasped by the pain of primal rejection and by the power of God to face this. The adoptee may be at risk spiritually because he or she may shrink from being grasped by anything, choosing instead to avoid being at a deeper level in order to avoid the *literal* nonbeing of a lost portion of one's self. (Remember Tillich's definition of neurosis.) It may make sense to adoptees to shut away their painful sagas of relinquishment and avoid the fuller demands of being itself: mourning, identity confusion, intimacy ex-pectations, and fantasy resolution.

Finally, as Tillich sees it, there are some positive things to say about de-spair. The depths of life's potential pain and meaninglessness are not to be avoided, but embraced. Here, again, one encounters the God beyond God. "The acceptance of despair is in itself faith and on the boundary line of the courage to be."[22] The acceptance of the reality of despair may be a rather precise definition of the moment of rebirth for the adoptee. It may mean being born again in the face of God who empowers the adoptee to move beyond the walls of nonbeing, the closed files of birth stories, toward some-thing new, something yet to be discovered as a future that can embrace a tarnished little bracelet—a painful past. "The threat of nonbeing makes God a living God."[23]

The representational world of the adoptee, as with all of us, is a world of many pictures of God. These are ideas constructed sometimes to save a partial sense of self, but sometimes they defeat the living God. It is only when one's true story is finally told in all its nonbeing painfulness and only in accepting the deepest truths about ourselves, that real being, real living is discovered. In the very face of death we find life. Following the cross of suffering is the resurrection to being. Put differently, accepting our own spiritual distress may lead to reconstructing images of God which, according to Tillich, may approximate the real God beyond God. A bracelet may bind us to God.

The Importance of Reexperiencing

Pastoral care and counseling may be a critical part of the life experience of adoptees that helps them to reconfigure the reality of God. Certainly and obviously not all relinquished and adopted people need help with God nor do they necessarily need counseling. The bonds of adoptive relationships may sufficiently mitigate the circumstances of abandonment as it is experienced in relinquishment. This is always the hope when adoption occurs. But for some, the strength of adoptive connection is not enough. These adoptees may need help to successfully manage relinquishment, to find God to be a good God. Here the support and the care of pastors and congregations as well as the help of pastoral psychotherapy may be critical to their reexperiencing God in a different way. Understanding the realities of adoptive development as they have been outlined can equip pastors, families, and congregations in the task of helping adoptees see the caring hand of God coming toward them, not going away from them—coming toward them to engage them in the midst of their lonely feelings, in the midst of their questioning God and the seemingly severe limits of God's goodness. Otherwise, as with other forms of the human dilemma, relinquishment and adoption may be an experience in which a human being—a *little* human being—is at risk in terms of being sufficiently grasped by the gracious hand of God.

Chapter Eight

Relinquishment and Belonging: A Pastoral and Ethical Reflection

*This is what the Sovereign LORD says to Jerusalem: Your ancestry
and birth were in the land of the Canaanites; your father was an
Amorite and your mother a Hittite. On the day you were born your
cord was not cut, nor were you washed with water to make you clean,
nor were you rubbed with salt or wrapped in cloths. No one looked on
you with pity or had compassion enough to do these things for you.
Rather, you were thrown out into the open field, for on the day you
were born you were despised.*

*Then I passed by and saw you kicking about in your blood, and as you
lay there in your blood I said to you, "Live!" I made you grow like a
plant of the field. You grew up and developed and became the most
beautiful of jewels. . . . I gave you my solemn oath and entered into a
covenant with you, declares the Sovereign LORD, and you became mine.*

—The prophet Ezekiel (16:3–8)

This book has been about belonging. Perhaps nothing in life matters more.
In terms of important and even ultimate concerns in our lives, belonging
may be the most critical of human experiences. Unless a child belongs at
the beginning of life, it may not even survive. Infant deaths at the Tavistock Clinic and the Hampstead Nurseries outside of London in World War
II days were sometimes ascribed to unknown reasons. Babies lost hope because no one "passed by and picked them up." There was no one to whom
they belonged, and they simply died. "Failure to thrive," the term used, offers no explanation. Each of us needs to belong to someone.

The people of Israel were like an infant cast off into an open field. No one claimed them. Then God announces their identity to them, offering them the truth about their genetic history. He speaks to them the reality of their relinquishment: that no one was there for them, to take pity and have compassion and clean them up for living. And then God, the adoptive parent, steps in to make his claim. He picked up the infant child and cut its cord, which lay beside it in the field. And he washed her. And he brought her up to be a "jewel among jewels." And he announced to all the world the all-important words: "You are mine!"

Unless we belong to someone, a very precious part of ourselves, our very soul, begins to die. Belonging is the conscious experience of another's deep investment in us. Unless there is another being (an "object" in the theoretical language of psychology, or a "person" in the language of everyday life) who is just plain crazy about us, we as humans are denied the opportunity to be fully planted on earth or fully grounded in heaven. The nature and severity of character disorders depends, we believe, in part on the limitations set on *belonging* in early life. If bonding to caregivers is insufficient, there is a price to pay in terms of how much capacity for attachment can develop. Unless God is seen as caring, unless God is pictured as stepping in to wash us up and claim us, the human spirit suffers defeat. The first question of the Heidelberg Catechism catches the importance of this connection to another when, in response to the inquiry about our greatest comfort in life and in death, it answers: "That I am not my own but I *belong* to my faithful Savior Jesus Christ."[1] Somebody must love us, we must belong to someone, if we are to be well.

Waiting to Belong

Despite all the efforts of caring adoptive parents who certainly lay claim to their children and offer a place to belong, adoptees are people who both belong and don't belong. This may, to some degree, be the case for all of us, given the complexities of human relationships, but in a special way adoptees may believe that they really belong to their birth parents and that they belong to their adoptive parents in name and in structure more than in substance, the substance of who they are. Nancy Verrier suggests that adoptees are people who are still "waiting to belong." Their developmental path is complex because, in fact, they belong in differing ways to two sets of parents. She writes that the relinquished and adopted child must

cope with the unnatural state of living in one family while biologically belonging to another. How can he feel as if he belongs in a house full of strangers? After all, few aspects of his being seem to be reflected in these

people. . . . Belong is a loaded word for adoptees. Although the adopted
child is told that he belongs to his adoptive parents, he doesn't really feel
as if this is true. Belonging is something that he never feels. He is yearn-
ing for it. Belonging is what he is searching for when he begins to search
for his birth family.[2]

To whatever degree this is the case for adoptees, it certainly makes belonging a central issue in their lives. Developmentally, of course, belonging
is an issue for all of us in terms of growing up healthy. But many of us in the
nonadopted world can *assume* that we belong. It's different for adoptees.
The clear belief that one is forever connected to another is not easy to accept when life begins with relinquishment. The unfortunate disruption of
relinquishment may set in motion a powerful corrective drive to restore oneself to the "original state of belonging" by always, at some level, being in
search of the persons that were lost in the beginning. The reason that
adoptees search, when they do, for their birth parents is most likely *more*
than the need for medical history, *more* than the need to know what parents
and siblings look like, *more* than the need even to learn that these ghost people are all right. The greatest need in searching may be the need to belong.

In an article entitled "Why Adoptees Search," psychologists Mary Krueger
and Fred Hanna make this point. They view the search for birth parents as a
variation of what they consider to be "universal concerns around death, isolation, meaninglessness, being, anxiety and freedom."

> The motivation appears to be an attempt to ground oneself in the reality
> of one's origins and form a conceptualization from which one can con-
> struct one's own reality-based adoption story. The pervasive theme in all
> this is a fundamental striving for *a sense of belonging*.[3]

Adoptees, in the midst of the emotional and spiritual struggle with relinquishment, may have been hurt in a very sacred place in their souls where
uncertainty about belonging to someone keeps an ache alive. It is a pain that
may be only partially relieved with the knowledge and the *experience* of
bringing these people into reality. Because belonging matters so much.

Bret is an example of an adoptee who struggled to belong. He came for
pastoral counseling for a variety of reasons. His grades were poor because
he had no motivation to study, reporting that at school he "just did not fit
in." He suffered from a depression that he had refused to acknowledge. At
age fifteen he was hospitalized because he was suicidal. Despite the good
efforts of his adoptive parents to care, he could not be convinced that he
belonged. He wrote this short story for his eleventh-grade English teacher:

> I sat on the bench outside the pet store one afternoon. Inside the window
> was a precious puppy. It was the only one left. I sat for a good thirty min-
> utes and in that time not one person stopped to gaze or peer through the

frosted glass at the puppy. And then she came. A small, very little girl. She was keeping a steady pace, slow and relaxed. And when she approached the window, she caught a glimpse out of the corner of her eye. She was paralyzed by what she saw. She turned to face the puppy head on. I was intrigued so I continued to observe. Her eyes were locked on the young pup. The girl slowly moved closer to the glass and reluctantly touched it with her soft hand. Like an elevator, her hand proceeded up and descended down again, carving delicate lines through the frost. I knew what she was thinking; I could feel it. She, as I once did, stood in awe. For she wasn't looking in the glass; she was looking in a mirror. I was there before too. The puppy, the girl and I have something in common. We are together, part of a family. We're not a minority or ethnic group; we just have all shared the same experience. We have all experienced abandonment and separation. I've been where the puppy is. So has she. Waiting to be claimed. Waiting to be loved. Waiting. The gazing came to an abrupt end. My gazing at her, her at the dog. The young Asian girl was whisked away by a white woman. The woman that the girl had learned to call mom.

Waiting to belong. It is something that all of us do to some degree. Bret, in all of his adolescent acting out, was letting the world know, as the story tells, that he felt that he did not belong. He needed a place to be himself, to belong to someone *for keeps*. When he was able to put this dilemma in words he began to see the limits of his belonging to people. And, of course, when he was able to become more realistic about the issue of belonging to someone, he began to belong *more* to his adoptive parents, the people in his life who cared.

Among the Sioux of centuries ago there was a common practice of providing every son and daughter with a second father and a second mother at birth. Usually these were friends of the "blood" parents who had taken an oath to care for the child in addition to the care provided by its biological parents.[4] Sioux children grew up aware that there were more than two people involved in their care, more than two people to whom they *belonged*. They were claimed by others, emotionally connected to them as well. Adoptees know about this. Like the children of the Sioux, the children of adoption belong to many people. They too have connections to other parents, but they have not been claimed by them. And, quite understandably, they often wish to reconnect to make their stories and their lives complete.

Pastoral Dimensions of Belonging

What happens when your parents are not your ancestors? What forms of pastoral care are indicated for those who struggle with the ghost parent phenomenon? What helps? The answers to these questions have to do with fostering a sense of belonging as a theme of ministry to relinquished and adopted people. There may be a particularly positive response to relating because it is so meaningful, or a particularly cautious response because much is at stake. But, in either circumstance, the basic shepherding dimensions of care are required in response to the pain that adoptees sometimes bring to the counseling office.

To belong is, first of all, to be claimed. Just as the people of Old Testament Israel were claimed by Jehovah, so each of us needs parents who claim us as their own. Without this unique form of ownership a sense of belonging does not occur. Adoptive parents may sometimes struggle with not sufficiently claiming their children as their own, but no matter how well they do so, the adoptee is still in part *unclaimed* by the ghost parents of personal history. This is a point of unusual sensitivity. Accordingly, sometimes in pastoral counseling with relinquished and adopted children giving them a sense of "being claimed" as a counselee can be a powerful tool of change. With these children, something like a postcard from a vacation trip may be meaningful in terms of facilitating the sense of being important *to* the counselor. Sometimes, with relinquished and adopted adults, attending to and interpreting the wish to be claimed or adopted by the counselor will be an important part of good pastoral care. Ownership of the counseling relationship by the counselor, in the good sense of sincere investment in caring and helping, will be especially critical to moving ministry to adoptees forward toward the depth of trust necessary to facilitate change.

To belong means, among other things, to be understood. Belonging to another includes being known "in one's innermost being" by that person. But, as this book has demonstrated, adoptees in our society have been far from understood in terms of the realities of relinquishment. Adoption law and adoption practice have not been guided by an appreciation of the unique difficulties that come with relinquishment or by the civil and human rights of adoptees to know their true stories. When adoptees are seen through the filter of "who they are supposed to be" in the eyes of adoptive parents and society at large, they are in fact *not* truly seen for "who they are." They are persons with unique and sometimes complex developmental challenges. If these challenges go unappreciated, then adoptees, even in the process of pastoral counseling, may never feel as if they belong in the room. And then in counseling they reexperience the subtle sting of "not quite belonging" that may have been the story of childhood. Belonging cannot happen without understanding, and adoptees are especially at risk in terms of not being understood by counselors.

Belonging also means being appreciated. When we belong to someone, we have a sense that not only are we claimed and understood, but we are also enjoyed. The idea that we, with all of our strengths and weaknesses, bring pleasure to another is the blessing that we bring to belonging. The mirroring that is part of good pastoral care, especially as this relates to noticing the real goodness of people and the value of their gifts and skills, will be especially important to the adoptee. No matter how kindly and gently we might want to say it, the adoptee's *experience* was that he was not of great enough value to be kept, to belong in the first place. *Being adopted is about second-place belonging, no matter how good the second place may be.* There is usually a question of value and sometimes a sense of shame as part of the self of the adoptee. Belonging that shows itself in the sincere enjoyment of the adoptee, the honest appreciation of whatever she has to bring to the story of living, is healing.

Belonging, finally, for our purposes, has also to do with defending. If we belong and we are under a threat of some form, belonging means there will be advocacy and even defense. To belong is to be fought over, even died for. This is the core of the gospel. Jesus died for the people who belong to him. And this is where the story of relinquishment and adoption takes a political turn. To the degree that belonging is the theme for ministry to adoptees, it may be that joining in the fight for their human right to know their medical records, personal stories, and birth parents is essential to good pastoral care.

In a discussion of the First and Fourth Amendments to the Constitution, Rich Uhrlaub asks the question:

> How far can the government intervene in the lives of adults who are not a known threat to each other? Phrased another way, does the government have the right to seize the personal papers of citizens and tell them with whom they may or may not associate? When applied to virtually any non-criminal life situation other than adoption, the answer is embarrassingly clear.[6]

As we have seen, adoptees are at political and societal disadvantage in many ways. Coming to their defense in order to bring balance to the inequity of human rights among adoptees, birth parents, and adoptive parents is part of the challenge of ministry to create belonging. Justice itself can be therapeutic.

Ethical Concerns around Relinquishment

The great problem with the subject of relinquishment and adoption in American society is that, ultimately, it has to do with sex, the act of intercourse—illicit sex that results in pregnancy as well as sex within the boundaries of an infertile marriage. Both are usually painful experiences that may lend themselves to a variety of defensive denials. In other cultures it may be different. In many economically marginalized American communities, extended family members often take over parenting when birth parents are unable to do so. But in middle- and upper-class American culture, at least until the last few years, families having the financial means to do otherwise have been less inclined to take on this responsibility themselves. Thus relinquishment and adoption have been associated with secrecy and denial because, in the dominant American social context, families have been both eager and able to avoid the practical consequences of illicit sex. Accordingly, infants have been more quickly put up for adoption, covering both the social stigma of illicit sex and the embarrassment of infertility.

These are critically important considerations because the secrecy and denial that have historically been part of American society also mutated into a certain blindness to some basic human and Christian values. How we place values on certain behaviors—how we think about what people do—has much to do with our responses to them, especially in pastoral counseling work. And, of course, the culture that we are part of always informs our thinking and our judgments to some degree. Our truest response to the needs of those in the adoption triad is determined by our own values in regard to their behaviors. Try as we might to be neutral, our values, both personal and societal, play an important role in the content and the method of our pastoral response. And fifty years ago our societal attitudes about intercourse outside of wedlock and our responses to women (not the men) who "got caught" set the stage for many of the problems that we face today in terms of offering help to triad members.

In Oklahoma City, nearly thirty years ago, there was a home for unwed mothers called the "Home of Redeeming Love." It was anything but that. Like many such homes of its day, it was the long-distance destination for pregnant girls who had been "sent" there to deliver their babies, relinquish them, and then return the hundreds of miles to home, acting "as if" the pregnancy and delivery and relinquishment never happened, trying to believe that they could go on in life as if nothing had happened. In fact, pregnant girls "redeemed themselves" by sacrificing their children. Many at the home had been told by angry, judgmental parents that they could not return home if they chose to keep their babies. The cost for illicit sex was the price of a child. That was the harsh judgment of American society against the sexual behavior of its children.

Within this historical setting, relinquishment certainly made sense. The child was "freed" of its status as an "illegitimate child" (though really only parents can be illegitimate). The amended birth certificate removed the (ink) stain of the term "bastard," literally stamped on the original document. The child was saved from a future of judgment. The birth parents, mothers mostly, though they endured the shaming of society and hospital nurses and doctors during pregnancy and delivery, were "freed" to return home without the ongoing rejection and discriminating comments that went with single parenting. And adoptive parents, many wanting children by adoption because they were nonconceptive, were given children "as if" by birth. They were also legally protected in anonymity from unwanted intrusions by birth parents, who could potentially interfere with their families as well as remind them of the painful truth of infertility. So it looked like a "win" for all three triad members. At that time in history, 95 percent of single Anglo mothers relinquished their babies. It appeared to serve the best interests of all.

But shame-based decisions always have their down side. They facilitate denial. When threatened by judgment against the sin, the shameful act of illicit sex, or the embarrassment of unfruitful sex, these decisions to make believe press people toward the illusion that nothing ever happened. Precisely at this point their choices become potentially pathogenic. The world of make-believe, although a good place for children to play, becomes the land of escape for adults. All of the triad members have indeed lost someone. The birth parents lost the child. The child lost the birth parents. The adoptive parents lost the child never delivered in birth. And to make believe, to deny these losses and the reality of the losses of these ghost people, because of the shame of nonmarital sex or the disappointment of infertility, is to inevitably set the stage for further denial of several basic values of civil Christian living. Five in particular come to mind.

Human Responsibility

It is a matter of human responsibility to give a child a name, an address, a history, a place in the universe. But the weight of shame was so heavy years ago that it blinded our moral eyes to the importance of taking responsibility for our sexual deeds. We as a society thought it better to let birth parents "off the hook" of human responsibility. It is one thing to confess and be forgiven; it is quite another to not be held accountable. It may well be that no sperm or egg donors ought ever leave their genetic codes for a child without leaving an always current name and address and telephone number. Sperm are not simply sperm; they are half of the blueprints of persons. Eggs are not just eggs; they are the cradles of humanity. Conception is a sacred moment; God acts in the creation of a person.

Not holding parents accountable for conceiving a child, at least at the level of clarity about who they are and how they are and where they are, is to deny a human responsibility, which inevitably puts the child of not-known parents at a disadvantage. Again, it conveys responsibility to offer a child a name, an ethnicity, an accurate medical history, a birthmark in the pages of a person's life. Shame can be sinister in that it may compromise the importance and the spiritual benefit of taking responsibility. (Running from the results of a pregnancy may mean a life of running from the presence of God.) The adoptee, because of the shame of another, has been left not known and not knowing. Keeping responsibility in place in relinquishment and adoption is keeping a basic human value where it belongs.

Justice

Adoptees have a civil and human right to know their stories, including the reality of their ghost parents. For those of us in the nonadopted world, for example, our birth certificates are free for the asking. Depending on the state in which the birth occurred, most adoptees must pay significant fees to begin the legal process of creating the *possibility* of retrieving their original birth certificates. Although this may not be an issue for many adoptees who choose not to search or do not feel that they need to know this information, the idea of justice would suggest that, certainly as adults, they have a right to know . . . just as the rest of us do.

The fact that today there are thousands of genetically related medical conditions, not known years ago, adds to the weight of justice for adoptees in terms of knowing medical histories. When Bethany learned of her breast cancer and the cancerous invasion of sixteen of twenty-two lymph nodes, she was angered at not knowing her medical history. If she had been diagnosed more quickly, treatment would have been less invasive and her prognosis for the future improved. She has a right to know even without all the advances in the field of medicine. It is unfair to put any human being at a disadvantage when other methods of dealing with problems are available that would mitigate inequity. But the voice of the infant adoptee, making a claim for fairness, could not be heard. Unfortunately, dealing with the issue of shame stopped society from thinking more carefully about long-term issues of justice for the children of relinquishment.

Truth

Honesty is a basic human principle that society employs to guide human interactions. But with regard to relinquishment and adoption, historically American society has not been honest. Birth certificates did not tell the truth. Many adoptees were told untrue stories about the death of birth parents in order to "bring closure" to relinquishment. Pregnant unwed mothers were given aliases, supposedly to protect their identity. But it was not honest. In the era of homes for unwed mothers, the practice of relinquishment and adoption was not guided by the importance of telling the truth; instead it was a collusion of dishonesty and secrecy that, ironically, reinforced the very shame it was intended to nullify.

God is a god of truth, truth about who God is and truth about who we

are, with all of our strengths and weaknesses, all of our goodness and bad-
ness. And such truth is liberating, taking us away from the tyranny of a
painful past. But the truth that could set the adoptee free, and could set the
birth parent free, and could set the adoptive parent free was held captive to
concerns about shame and embarrassment . . . and no one was set free. Making believe with the truth can be a dangerous thing to do when the future
well-being of all the members of the triad is at stake. When the fear of
shame is so powerful as to subvert the importance of honesty, then the sins
of the fathers and the mothers are visited upon their children in a way that
stops life from being the blessing that it can be—a life free from shame. The
truth about relinquishment years ago would have set many adoptees free
today in a way that they have not yet been free.

Human Dignity

Shame always compromises dignity, both internally, in terms of the self-
evaluation of a person, and externally, in terms of how people view a person. It is a process that takes away the value of a person. Birth parents, birth
mothers especially, may experience a significant loss of their own dignity,
especially if they have been scorned by parents, by social workers, by nurses
in the delivery room, and, in their own way of thinking, by God. Being
treated as "less than," because of their breaks with what were the moral
codes of society, may have been costly in terms of the loss of human dignity. And adoptees are parts of these parents, sometimes carrying shame "to
the third and the fourth generation."

And yet the dignity of each person as a citizen and a child of God is a basic value intended to guide our decisions about dealing with people. This
dignity needs to be maintained as much as is possible in difficult situations—like single pregnancy for the birth parent and relinquishment for
the adoptee and adoption for the adoptive parent—because, among other
things, each needs a sense of personal dignity to function well in the face of
their unique challenges. Shame is sinister in that it drains people of their
dignity and leads to despair. But in the practice of relinquishment and
adoption years ago, the importance of preserving human dignity was lost in
the anxious battle against the sexual impulse.

Reconciliation

Underlying relinquishment and adoption is the agony that may accompany human separation. When two hearts are closely bound, when the prenatal infant hears the sounds of its mother's heartbeat and the song or the
sadness in her voice, then postnatal, lifelong separation may be an injury
too awful to know. We may never be certain about such injury, but nevertheless we should address the concern about *unnecessary* suffering within the

context of relinquishment and adoption, to minimize the suffering of all those who struggle within the adoption triad.

Reconciliation as a theme for ministry and care has always been a hallmark of the church community. Bringing together the alienated, resolving conflicts where emotions have been injured, making peace where there has been war—this is the meaning of reconciliation. The adoptee's heart must be reconciled to the reality of relinquishment and the actual difficulties of adoption. If such "heart reconciliation" occurs, as this book has outlined it, then life can be good, then joy in living and loving can become reality. But without reconciliation, as much as it is possible, the heart of the adoptee remains unmended. Life is diminished and shame has its way. Reconciling adoptees to their personal truths, to their birth parents, to their God is all part of what must happen for the story to have a better ending. The idea that such reconciliations are not necessary may have made the secrecy and deceit of relinquishment go more easily years ago, but today such thinking stops the adoptee from living a life that is characterized by honesty, self-understanding, self-acceptance, and hope. The "bringing together" inherent in the word *reconciliation* is the antidote to the suffering that shame can create. Reconciliation means a reconnection to ghost parents that makes them real, no longer ghosts in the adoptee's story. It means finding the lost pearl of great price—personhood, claimed and reconciled as one of the greater gifts of God.

Back to the Garden

In Eden, as the Bible story goes, we were all relinquished, rejected in the birthplace of humanity, given away to the earth. We were thrown out at the gate to suffer in a world hurt from its beginning. But God is the birth parent who changed his mind and wanted us back. He decided not to be a ghost parent. And so we were given our names and reclaimed; our cords to dying were cut and we were cleaned up for living—unrelinquished. This is the gospel. And since that day of reclamation, humankind has always been going back to the garden. Because the garden is our birthplace, the earth of our identities. We belong to someone there; we belong to God. The garden is the source of our self-knowledge, of knowing who we are and where we came from. It is also the place where we risk getting close to other human beings, the Eden where we sometimes dare to walk in our nakedness and take pleasure in loving and being loved by another. Our dreams become reality there, so we dream again and embrace the goodness of living. And in the garden, with God, is the place of our hoping, hoping that our futures will bloom in pastures yet to be discovered. In the garden our humanity is restored by God . . . as is the humanity of every adoptee.

Notes

Introduction: The Adoptee's Story

1. This term is taken from Nancy Verrier, *The Primal Wound: Understanding the Adopted Child* (Baltimore: Gateway Press, 1993). The author is an adoptive mother who describes the difficulties she experienced in parenting her adolescent daughter. Her term "the primal wound" is used to describe the break between the relinquished child and its birth mother.

2. See Betty Jean Lifton, *Journey of the Adopted Self: A Quest for Wholeness* (New York: Basic Books, 1994), esp. chap. 15, "The Mark of Oedipus."

3. In her book, *The Journey of The Adopted Self: A Quest for Wholeness* (Basic Books, 1994), Betty Jean Lifton develops the idea of a "Ghost Kingdom" (p. 57), the psychological place to which the adoptee, via imagination, retreats in order to maintain contact with the lost but real other family members. These include the ghosts of birth parents and birth siblings as well as the ghost of the "lost baby"—the child the adoptee would have been if raised by birth parents. These images are not known but nevertheless real members of the adoptee's family story. She calls it "an awesome sphere, located only in the adoptee's psychic reality," which, unfortunately, necessitates the task of living a "double life," one inside the adoptive family and one outside.

4. Studies include R. W. Toussieng, "Thoughts Regarding the Etiology of Psychological Difficulties in Adopted Children," *Child Welfare* 41 (1962): 59–71; N. M. Simon and A. G. Senturia, "Adoption and Psychiatric Illness," *American Journal of Psychiatry* 122 (1966): 858–68; L. Tec, "The Adopted Child's Adaptation to Adolescence," *Journal of Orthopsychiatry* 37 (1967): 402; A. Weiss, "Symptomolgy of Adopted and Non-adopted Adolescents in a Psychiatric Hospital," *Adolescence* 20, no. 80 (1985): 763–74; N. Senior and E. Himadi, "Emotionally Disturbed, Adopted, Inpatient Adolescents," *Child Psychiatry and Human Development* 15, no. 3 (1985): 189–97; C. S. Fullerton, et al., "Adoption Predicts Psychiatric Treatment Resistances in Hospitalized Adolescents," *Journal of American Academy of Child Psychiatry* 25, no. 4 (1986): 542–51.

5. P. M. Brinich and E. Brinich, "Adoption and Adaptation," *Journal of Nervous and Mental Diseases* 170, no. 8 (1982): 147–65.

6. Mary Sue Kendrick, "The Journey to Become Real," *Roots and Wings* (winter 1991): 3–7.

7. Larry Kent Graham, "From Psyche to System," *Theology Today* 49, no. 3 (October 1992): 328. See his text *Care of Persons, Care of Worlds* (Nashville: Abingdon Press, 1992) for a creative discussion of creating balance between the treatment of the individual and the treatment of the individual's forming environment.

8. Lifton employs this term in *Journey of the Adopted Self.* See n. 2, chap. 1, here.

9. Paul Brinich, "Some Potential Effects of Adoption on Self and Object Representations," *The Psychoanalytic Study of the Child*, 35 (New Haven, Conn.: Yale University Press, 1980), 107–33.

Chapter 1. Hearing a Dissonant Echo: The Adoptee as a Person

1. The phrase "split-life experience" is taken from Lifton's book *Journey of the Adopted Self*, in which she describes how adoptees draw their identities from both sides of the stories of relinquishment and adoption. She maintains that this is a lifelong experience for the adoptee. The complex difficulty of living with two sets of parents is never finally resolved into an experience of wholeness; it is a "split life" that is managed and lived with, but not resolved into oneness.

2. Brinich, "Some Potential Effects of Adoption," 107–33.

3. Rickie Solinger, *Wake Up Little Susie: Single Pregnancy and Race before Roe v. Wade* (New York: Routledge, Chapman & Hall, 1992). This text provides the first published analysis of maternity home programs for unwed mothers between 1945 and 1965.

4. Betty Jean Lifton, *Lost and Found: The Adoptive Experience* (New York: Harper & Row, 1979), esp. chap. 9, "Good Adoptee—Bad Adoptee."

5. The adoptive development video *More Than Love* (Grand Rapids: Bethany Productions, 1992) is a fifty-five-minute documentary that describes how love from adoptive parents is not enough for complete adoptive development. The video presents relationships in fantasy and reality with birth parents as part of the mix of development.

6. Thomas Verny, M.D., *The Secret Life of the Unborn Child* (New York: Bantam Books, 1981), esp. chap. 3, "The Prenatal State of Self," and chap. 4, "Intrauterine Bonding."

7. Ronald J. Nydam, "Hope and Fantasy in the Lives of Searching Adopted Adults: A Qualitative Study," dissertation, 1994, University of Denver and the Iliff School of Theology, UMI Dissertation Services, Ann Arbor, Michigan, order no. 9429764.

8. Florence Clothier, "The Psychology of the Adopted Child," *Mental Hygiene* (1943): 230.

9. See Arthur D. Sorosky, Annette Baran, and Reuben Pannor, *The Adoption Triangle—Sealed or Open Records: How They Affect Adoptees, Birth Parents, and Adoptive Parents* (San Antonio: Corona Publishing Co., 1984).

10. *The Orphan Trains*, produced and directed by Janet Graham and Edward Gray, PBS Home Video, 1995.

11. Ibid.

Chapter 2. The Necessary Mourning of Relinquishment

1. During the '50s and '60s the Salvation Army instituted many homes by that name in major cities across America to care for single pregnant women. The intent was benevolent, but the experience of being shunned by society, kept a secret, and whisked away to these places was often demeaning and painful.

2. Verny, *Secret Life of the Unborn Child*, 32.

3. Ibid.; see esp. chap. 3, "The Prenatal Self," and chap. 4, "Intrauterine Bonding."

4. Ibid., 35. Verny writes: "Freud's work touched only briefly on the unborn child. Traditional neurological and biological opinion in his day held that

a child was not mature enough to feel or experience meaningfully until the second or third year of life, which is why he too thought that personality did not begin developing until then."

5. The idea of self-awareness, especially as it relates to identity formation, will be discussed in detail in chap. 3.

6. Ibid., 59.

7. Ibid., 87.

8. Verrier, *Primal Wound*, 1.

9. Ibid., 21.

10. Ibid., 70.

11. David M. Brodzinsky, Leslie M. Singer, and Anne M. Braff, "Children's Understandings of Adoption," *Child Development* 55 (1984): 869–78.

12. Ibid., 871–72.

13. Ibid., 872.

14. Marshall D. Schechter, M.D., "Observations on Adopted Children," *Archives of General Psychiatry* 3 (1960): 45–56, 58.

15. Herbert Wieder, M.D., "On When and Whether to Disclose about Adoption," *Journal of American Psychoanalytic Association* 36 (1978): 793–811, esp. 795.

16. Thomas Brosnan, S.J., "Coming of Age: Toward a Spirituality of Adoption," *American Adoption Congress Decree* 3 (fall 1996): 3, 15.

17. Steven L. Nickman, "Losses in Adoption: The Need for Dialogue," *Psychoanalytic Study of the Child* 40 (New Haven, Conn.: Yale University Press, 1985), 365–98.

18. Ibid., 371.

Chapter 3. Adoptee Identity: The Fruit of Two Trees

1. Brinich, "Some Potential Effects of Adoption," 107.

2. D. W. Winnicott, *The Child, the Family, and the Outside World* (New York: Penguin Books, 1964), 17.

3. Margaret Mahler, Fred Pine, and Andrew Bergman, *The Psychological Birth of the Human Infant* (New York: Basic Books, 1975). These authors suggest that the self-awareness of the child occurs as late as at fifteen to eighteen months of age.

4. M. D. S. Ainsworth and B. Wittig, "Attachment and Exploratory Behavior in One-Year-Olds in a Stranger Situation," in *Determinants of Infant Behavior*, ed. B. M. Foss (New York: Wiley Press, 1969).

5. Daniel N. Stern, *The Interpersonal World of the Human Infant* (New York: Basic Books, 1985), 39.

6. Ibid., 10.

7. Ibid., 26.

8. D. W. Winnicott, "Two Adopted Children," in *The Child and the Outside World: Studies in Developing Relationships* (London: Tavistock Publications, 1957), 54. Here Winnicott makes a very similar point about the possibility of early experience for the adopted infant as being one of significant awareness that results in a confusion that is life altering and sometimes difficult to tolerate.

9. Stern, *Interpersonal World*, 201.

10. Ibid., 204.

11. Brinich, "Some Potential Effects of Adoption," 107–33.

12. Ibid., 108.

13. H. J. Sants, "Genealogical Bewilderment in Children with Substitute Parents," *British Journal of Medical Psychology* 37 (1964): 133–41.

14. This story is told by Betty Jean Lifton in *Journey of the Adopted Self*, 205–6.

15. See, e.g., Rita Rogers, "The Adolescent and the Hidden Parent," *Comprehensive Psychiatry* 10, no. 4 (1969): 296–301; Arthur Sorosky, M.D., et al., "Identity Conflicts in Adoptees," *American Journal of Orthopsychiatry* (1975): 1, 18–27; Richard B. Feiertag, M.D., et al., "Identity Development in Adopted Children," *Pediatrics* 47 (1971): 5, 948–49; Max Frisk, "Identity Problems and Confused Conceptions of the Genetic Ego in Adopted Children during Adolescence," *Folkhalsans Tonarspoliklinik Helsinki* 74 (1988): 6–12; and Melissa Norvell and Rebecca F. Guy, "A Comparison of Self-Concept in Adopted and Non-adopted Adolescents," *Adolescence* 47 (1977): 443–47.

16. Lifton, *Lost and Found*, 54–61.

17. Ibid., 59.

18. See Robert S. Andersen, "The Nature of Adoptee Search: Adventure, Cure, or Growth?" *Child Welfare* 68 (November–December 1989): 6, 623–32; Robert S. Andersen, "Why Adoptees Search: Motives and More," *Child Welfare* 67 (January–February 1988): 1, 115–19; Mary J. Jago Krueger and Fred J. Hanna, "Why Adoptees Search: An Existential Perspective," *Journal of Counseling and Development* 75 (January–February 1997): 195–202; Paul Sachdev, "Adoption Reunion and After: A Study of the Search Process and Experience of Adoptees," *Child Welfare* 71 (January–February 1992): 53–68; and Janet Rosenzweig-Smithy, "Factors Associated with Successful Reunions of Adult Adoptees and Biological Parents," *Child Welfare* 67 (September–October 1988): 411–22. Each of these articles discusses the usefulness of search behavior in terms of identity consolidation and a deeper sense of grounding in reality.

19. David M. Brodzinsky, Marshall D. Schechter, and Robin Marantz Henig, *Being Adopted: The Lifelong Search for Self* (New York: Doubleday, 1992), 79.

20. Quoted in the Rev. Thomas F. Brosnan, "Strengthening Families," an address to the National Maternity and Adoption Conference, San Antonio, Texas, 1996.

Chapter 4. Adoptee Intimacy: Heartache and Love

1. Here the question of "leading the client" comes into focus. It is not thought to be good clinical practice to "take" a counselee to an issue for his or her review. However, given the societal collusion of secrecy around relinquishment and adoption, and the adoptee's training that it is not to be discussed, it may well be that responsible clinical work means bringing it up for discussion at a time when the client may be able to hear it. Unless this issue is lifted up for review at some point in the counseling process, the necessary grieving and identity formation and fantasy resolution may not occur.

2. See my "Character Disorders: Where Faith and Healing Sometimes Fail," *Journal of Pastoral Care* 45, no. 2 (summer 1991): 135–47, in which I discuss some of the possible problems that lack of attachment may create in personality structure, especially as this relates to relinquishment and adoption.

3. John Bowlby, *Attachment* (New York: Basic Books, 1973), 27–28.

4. John Bowlby, *Loss, Sadness, and Depression* (New York: Basic Books, 1980), 8.

5. David Wurster, "Marriage: Crucible for Growth," *Journal of Pastoral Care* 37 (winter 1983): 4, 259. The author cites the work of August Y. Napier with Carl A. Whitaker, who develop this idea as it relates to the marital relationship in their book *The Family Crucible* (New York: Bantam Books, 1978).

6. For an interesting discussion of "genetic sexual attraction," see Lifton's chapter "The Mark of Oedipus," in *Journey of the Adopted Self*, 225–40. Also, see the discussion of this in Judith S. Gediman and Linda P. Brown, *Birthbond: Reunions between Birthparents and Adoptees* (Far Hills, N.J.: Horizon Press, 1989).

7. According to Lifton, *Journey of the Adopted Self*, 225–40, the term may have come from Barbara Gonyo, who reported her sexual attraction to her own birth son in an article entitled "Genetic Sexual Attraction," in *Decree* (the American Adoption Congress newsletter) 4, no. 2 (1987). See also Lifton's note on page 320.

Chapter 5. Ghost Parent Wonderings: The Challenge of Fantasy Resolution

1. Marlou Russell, "Meeting My Mother," *Adoptees in Search Newsletter* (July–August 1995): 1–2.

2. Eric Klinger, "The Power of Daydreams," *Psychology Today* 21, no. 2 (1987): 37.

3. Ibid., 38.

4. Ibid., 42. Other theorists, such as Robert Firestone, *The Fantasy Bond* (New York: Human Sciences Press, 1985), and George Serban, *The Tyranny of Magical Thinking* (New York: E. P. Dutton, 1982), consider fantasy formation a symptom of mental illness, a trap into which some people fall which, despite its temporary relief, is a maladaptive approach to reality, leaving one of the margins of reality instead of facing and accepting reality in all of its fullness. Each sounds the Freudian dictum to relinquish the wish and face the world without the illusion of God or any other fantasy of longed-for connection.

5. Ibid., 44.

6. Linda C. Mayes and Donald J. Cohen, "The Development of a Capacity for Imagination in Early Childhood," *Psychoanalytic Study of the Child* 47 (New Haven, Conn.: Yale University Press, 1992), 23.

7. Ibid., 24.

8. Ibid., 27–28.

9. Schlomith Cohen, "The Reality in Fantasy-Making," *Psychoanalytic Study of the Child* 44 (New Haven, Conn.: Yale University Press, 1989), 69.

10. Margery Williams, *The Velveteen Rabbit* (New York: Avon Books, 1975), 12–13.

11. Mary Sue Kendrick, "The Journey to Become Real," *Roots and Wings* (winter 1991): 3–7.

12. Sigmund Freud, "Family Romances (1908)," *Standard Edition* 9 (London: Hogarth Press; 1958), 236–41.

13. Herbert Weider, "The Family Romance Fantasies of Adopted Children," *Psychoanalytic Quarterly* 46 (1977): 185.

14. Ibid., 186.

15. Brinich, "Some Potential Effects of Adoption," 108.

16. Weider, "Family Romance Fantasies," 186.

17. Ibid., 187.

18. Object-relations theorists repositioned traditional psychoanalytic theory, placing much more emphasis on the beginnings of life, and also expanding the theory beyond its own boundaries, maintaining that the world of object relations, the infant's environment, forms the personality of the child just as much as the regulation of instinctual drives within. See Howard A. Bacal and Kenneth M. Newman, *Theories of Object-Relations: Bridges to Self-Psychology* (New York: Columbia University Press, 1990).

19. D. W. Winnicott, "The Ordinary Devoted Mother," in *Babies and Their Mothers*, ed. Claire Winnicott, Ray Shepherd, and Madeleine Davis (Reading, Mass: Addison-Wesley, 1987), 9–10.

20. D. W. Winnicott, "The Birth Experience," in *Human Nature*, ed. Claire Winnicott, Ray Shepherd, and Madeleine Davis (New York: Schocken Books, 1988), 143.

21. Ibid., 129.

22. Winnicott, "Two Adopted Children," 55.

23. Ibid., 64.

24. Ibid., 53.

25. D. W. Winnicott, "Transitional Objects and Transitional Phenomena," in *Playing and Reality* (New York: Basic Books, 1971), 2.

26. Madeleine Davis and David Wallbridge, *Boundary and Space: An Introduction to the Work of D. W. Winnicott* (New York: Brunner/Mazel, 1981), 44.

27. Winnicott, "Transitional Objects and Transitional Phenomena," 12.

28. Ibid., 3.

29. Alan Sugarman and Lee S. Jaffee, "A Developmental Line of Transitional Phenomena," in *Facilitating Environment: Clinical Applications of Winnicott's Theory*, ed. M. Gerard Fromm and Bruce L. Smith (Madison, Wis.: International Universities Press, 1989), 106.

30. D. W. Winnicott, "The Capacity to Be Alone," in *The Maturational Process and the Facilitating Environment* (London: Hogarth Press, 1965), 30.

31. For a summary of this dissertation study, see my "Fantasy and Hope in the Lives of Adoptees," *Journal of Pastoral Care* 51, no. 1 (spring 1997): 65–78. In its complete form it is available as "Hope and Fantasy in the Lives of Searching Adopted Adults: A Qualitative Study"; see n. 7, chap. 1, here.

32. Afro American, Native American, and Hispanic American subcultures hold different beliefs about relinquishment and adoption. In these groups the extended family plays a greater role in raising unplanned children. Relinquish-

ment is less common, and adoption may be seen as a task of the community, the village that raises the child.

33. Brodzinsky, et al., *Being Adopted*. These authors report that "100% of adoptees search, if only in their minds," p. 79. In their study of nearly one hundred adoptees they conclude that "in our experience . . . it may not be a literal search, but it is a meaningful search, nonetheless. It begins when the child first asks, 'Why did it happen?' 'Who are they?' 'Where are they now?'" p. 79. Their point is that extrafamilial adoption inevitably entails a psychic search of some form for "lost" birth parents.

34. D. W. Winnicott, "The Manic Defense," in *Collected Papers: Through Paediatrics to Psycho-analysis* (London: Tavistock Publications, 1958), 82.

35. Mayes and Cohen, "Development of a Capacity for Imagination," 26–27.

Chapter 6. Keeping Hope Alive: Despairing about Relinquishment

1. C. R. Snyder, Cheri Harris, and John Anderson, "The Will and the Ways: Development and Validation of an Individual Measure of Hope," *Journal of Personality and Social Psychology* 60, no. 4 (1991): 570. See also Dora and Erwin Panofsky, *Pandora's Box: The Changing Aspects of a Mythical Symbol* (New York: Harper & Row, 1965).

2. Karl Menninger, "Hope," *Bulletin of the Menninger Clinic* 51, no. 5 (1987): 450.

3. There are many ways to consider hope and hopefulness from a psychological perspective. The term is used here in a restricted fashion to refer to its theological dimensions. See Verna Carson, Karen L. Soeken, and Patricia M. Grimm, "Hope and Its Relationship to Spiritual Well-Being," *Journal of Psychology and Theology* 16, no. 2 (1988): 160.

4. Gabriel Marcel, *Homo Viator: An Introduction to the Metaphysic of Hope*, trans. Emma Craufurd (Chicago: H. Regnery Co., 1951), 32.

5. Paul Pruyser, "Maintaining Hope in Adversity," *Bulletin of the Menninger Clinic* 51, no. 5 (1987): 465.

6. Ibid.

7. James L. Muyskens, *The Sufficiency of Hope: Conceptual Foundations of Religion* (Philadelphia: Temple University Press, 1979), xi.

8. Ibid., 127.

9. Emil Brunner, *Faith, Hope, and Love* (Philadelphia: Westminster Press, 1956), 43–44; italics mine.

10. Ibid., 38

11. Carl E. Braaten, *The Future of God: The Revolutionary Dynamics of Hope* (New York: Harper & Row, 1969), 18.

12. Ibid., 36.

13. Jürgen Moltmann, "Religion, Revolution, and the Future," in *The Future of Hope: Essays by Bloch, Fackenheim, Moltmann, Metz, and Capps*, ed. Walter H. Capps (Philadelphia: Fortress Press, 1970), 103.

14. Ibid.

15. Ibid., 102.

16. Ibid., 122.

17. Andrew Lester, *Hope in Pastoral Care and Counseling* (Louisville, Ky.: Westminster John Knox Press, 1995). Lester shows that the development of "future stories" can be a method that enhances pastoral care by envisioning hopeful futures for persons in despair.

18. Gabriel Marcel, *Homo Viator*.

19. Ibid., 30.

20. Ibid.

21. Ibid., 32.

22. Ibid., 35.

23. Ibid.

24. Ibid., 54.

25. Ibid., 40.

26. Ibid., 67.

27. William F. Lynch, *Images of Hope: Imagination as Healer of the Helpless* (Notre Dame, Ind.: University of Notre Dame Press, 1974), 32.

28. Ibid., 229.

29. Ibid.

30. Ibid., 77.

31. Ibid., 35.

32. Ibid., 243.

33. Ibid., 169.

34. Ibid., 159–60. Lynch's comment correlates directly with the basic assumptions of object-relations theory, which holds that, in part, the person is formed, not only by intrapsychic process, but also by influence of relations to persons in the outside world. The presentation of Winnicott's thinking in the preceding chapter presents these assumptions.

35. Ibid., 23.

36. Ibid., 24.

37. Ibid., 160.

38. Ibid.

39. Ibid., 25.

40. Ibid., 24–25.

41. Lynch distinguishes himself from Freud in this regard. Whereas for Freud frustration of a wish is usually resolved via relinquishment of the wish, for Lynch the wish must be kept, albeit transformed into a longing for a realistic appropriate object. He critiques Freud as follows (p. 131):

> Freud sensed this problem, and he sensed his failure to resolve it. He tried at times to bring the wishing faculty of the libido and the organizing faculty of the ego into closer association. He protested that the boundaries of the one and the other should not be too carefully demarcated. Now and then he warned his fellow doctors not to take the monster picture of the wishing libido in such high seriousness and fear. But how to make the ego itself a daring, energizing, wishing entity seemed difficult for him. He looked ever so carefully for the origin of anxiety, locating it for the most part in the wishing of the libido or the instinctual drive of sexuality; *it never quite occurred to him that he should subject this whole system and turn it on its head, that it might be the failure to wish that produces*

anxiety. He was in touch with one form of the unconscious, the negative, destructive, and inhibiting world of repressed wishes for the inappropriate and
unreal. He rightly placed the seat of anxiety in the ego, but did he place it there
for a reason that was total enough? The self is indeed anxious because it feels
threatened by its own instincts. But is it not far more anxious because it feels
blocked thereby in its own capacity to wish, to love, to move on in its search
and hunger for reality? Does it then feel immobilized, unable to love? Is it not
anxious where it is not free?
Lynch's view of wishing is much more positive and less problematic than is Freud's
within the latter's rather negative anthropology.

42. Ibid., 141.
43. Ibid., 143.
44. Ibid., 177.
45. Ibid., 178–79.
46. Ibid., 213.
47. Ibid., 124.
48. Ibid., 190.
49. Ibid., 157.
50. Ibid., 58.
51. Marcel, *Homo Viator*, 53.

Chapter 7. Adoptees and God: A Variety of Images

1. This story (as well as the theoretical and theological perspectives found
in this chapter) was originally presented in my "Adoption and the Image of
God," *Journal of Pastoral Care* 46, no. 3 (fall 1992): 247–62.
2. Nickman, "Losses in Adoption," 371; italics mine.
3. Ana-Maria Rizzuto, *The Birth of the Living God* (Chicago: University of
Chicago Press, 1979), 7.
4. It is of interest to notice how Freud was unable to keep clear the line between science and religion, the demarcation between making a statement that
was psychological and making one that was theological. In *Moses and Monothe-
ism*, for example, he makes the case that the origins of religion have to do with
primitive struggles with infantile wishes that are not realistic and *therefore* he
concludes the idea of God is simply the projection of a wish. It is of the imagination. Whether God is real or not is not a question that psychology as psychology can ever address. The question is a theological inquiry.
5. Rizzuto, *Birth of the Living God*, 41.
6. Ibid., 46.
7. Ibid., 55.
8. Ibid., 87.
9. William W. Meissner writes in "Religious Thinking as Transitional
Conceptualization" (*Psychoanalytic Review* 79, no. 2 [1992]: 175–96) of the manner in which Rizzuto's ideas about God representations fit with the object-
relations formulations of transitional objects that serve in moving, transitioning
from one view of God to another. He writes (p. 188):

the God-representation is described as a form of transitional representation that the child, and later the adult, creates and sustains in the intermediate psychic space of illusory experience. Although it arises within the matrix of human subjectivity, it is not simply hallucinatory. The process by which the image of God is created as a personalized transitional representation continues throughout the life cycle.

10. Heinz Kohut, *The Analysis of the Self* (New York: International Universities Press, 1971), 25.

11. Ibid., 37.

12. Ibid., 25.

13. Ibid., 45.

14. Paul Tillich, *The Courage to Be* (New Haven, Conn.: Yale University Press, 1952), 4–5.

15. Ibid., 65.

16. Ibid., 105.

17. Paul Tillich, *The Dynamics of Faith* (New York: Harper & Row, 1957), 66.

18. Tillich, *Courage to Be*, 90.

19. Ibid., 39.

20. Ibid., 112.

21. Ibid., 85.

22. Ibid., 175.

23. Ibid., 180.

Chapter 8. Relinquishment and Belonging: A Pastoral and Ethical Reflection

1. Question and Answer #1, *The Heidelberg Catechism with Commentary* (Philadelphia: United Church Press, 1962), 17.

2. Nancy Verrier, "Addendum for Parents: Dual Identity, Behavior vs. Personality, Projective Identification," which Verrier offers to people who have read her book *The Primal Wound*. It offers further discussion about parenting relinquished and adopted children.

3. Mary J. Krueger and Fred J. Hanna, "Why Adoptees Search, An Existential Treatment Perspective," *Journal of Counseling and Development* 75 (January/February 1977): 195–202, see esp. 197; italics mine.

4. Mari Sandoz, *These Were the Sioux* (New York: Hastings House, 1961), 27.

5. Rich Uhrlaub, "The Crux of the Matter," *Good Cause: The Membership Letter of the American Adoption Congress* 1, no. 2 (April 1998): 13.

Index